Accession no.

KU-743-475

Ezra Pound and
the Making of Modernism

AMS STUDIES IN MODERN LITERATURE

ISSN 0270-2983

Set ISBN-13: 978-0-404-61570-3

No. 26

WILLIAM PRATT

EZRA POUND AND THE MAKING OF MODERNISM

ISBN-13: 978-0-404-61596-3

Ezra Pound and
the Making of Modernism

by William Pratt

LIS - LIBRARY

Date	Fund
30·03·16	XI·Shr

Order No.

2699047

University of Chester

AMS Press, Inc.
New York

Library of Congress Cataloging-in-Publication Data

Pratt, William, 1927–
 Ezra Pound and the Making of Modernism / William Pratt.
 p. cm. — (AMS Studies in Modern Literature, ISSN 0270-2983; no. 26)
 Includes bibliographical references and index.
 ISBN 13: 978-0-404-61596-3 (acid-free paper)
 1. Pound, Ezra, 1885–1972—Criticism and interpretation.
 2. Imagist poetry, American—History and criticism.
 3. Modernism (Literature) —United States.
 I. Title.

PS3531.O82Z7867   2007
811'.52—dc22   2007021636
                                                                 CIP

All AMS books are printed on acid-free paper that meets the guidelines for performance and durability of the Committee on Production Guidelines for Book Longevity of the Council on Library Resources.

Copyright © 2007 by AMS Press, Inc.
All rights reserved

AMS Press, Inc.
Brooklyn Navy Yard, 63 Flushing Ave. – Unit #221
Brooklyn, New York 11205-1005, USA
www.amspressinc.com

MANUFACTURED IN THE UNITED STATES OF AMERICA

FOR ANNE

always

ACKNOWLEDGMENTS

"Pound's Mutation: Translating Symbolism into Imagism" first appeared in *Ezra Pound, Dans le Vortex de la Traduction*, edited by Hélène Aji (Paris: Sorbonne, 2002). "Pound as Modern Troubadour" first appeared in *Ezra Pound and the Troubadours*, edited by Philip Grover (Gardonne, France: Editions Federop, 2000). "Pound and Yeats: The Poetics of Friendship" first appeared in *On Modern Poetry: Essays Presented to Donald Davie*, edited by Vereen Bell and Laurence Lerner (Nashville: Vanderbilt University Press, 1988). "The Greatest Poet in Captivity: Ezra Pound at St. Elizabeths" was first published in *The Sewanee Review* (Fall, 1986). "Pound's Hells, Real and Imaginary," first appeared in *Ezra Pound, Nature and Myth*, edited by William Pratt (New York: AMS Press, 2002).

Grateful acknowledgment is made to New Directions Publishing for permission to quote from the following works by Ezra Pound:

"Aegupton," "Histrion," "Li Bel Chasteus," "Redordillas, or Something of that sort," and "Scriptor Ignotus," from *Collected Early Poems* copyright ©1976 by The Ezra Pound Literary Property Trust. Reprinted by permission of New Directions Publishing Corp.

"Alba," "Ballad of the Goodly Fere," "Cino," "Exile's Letter," "He Speaks to the Moonlight Concerning the Beloved," "Homage to Sextus Propertius," "Hugh Selwyn Mauberley," "In a Station of the Metro," "La Fraisne," "Lament of the Frontier Guard," "Na Audiart," "Near Perigord," "O plasmatour and true celestial light...," "Piere Vidal Old," "The Lake Isle," "The Rest," "The Return," "The River-Merchant's Wife: A Letter," "The Spring," and "The Tree" from *Personae*, copyright ©1926 by Ezra Pound. Reprinted by permission of New Directions Publishing Corp.

"#181: To T. S. Eliot" (Sage Homme) from *Selected Letters of Ezra Pound*, copyright ©1950 by Ezra Pound. Reprinted by permission of New Directions Publishing Corp.

"Canto CXIII," "Canto CXVI," "Canto I," "Canto IV," "Canto LXXIII," "Canto LXXIV," "Canto LXXIX," "Canto LXXVI," "Canto LXXVII," "Canto LXXVII," "Canto LXXX" "Canto LXXXI," "Canto LXXXII," "Canto LXXXIII," "Canto LXXXIV," "Canto VII," "Canto XC," "Canto XI," and "Canto XXVI" from *The Cantos of Ezra Pound*, copyright ©1934, 1937, 1940, 1948, 1956, 1959, 1962, 1963, 1966, and 1968 by Ezra Pound. Reprinted by permission of New Directions Publishing Corp.

CONTENTS

PREFACE

Hypocrite lecteur,—mon semblable,—mon frère! Charles Baudelaire's shocking compliment to the readers of *Les Fleurs du Mal*, which he published Paris in 1857, was repeated by T. S. Eliot in *The Waste Land*, when he published his poem in London and New York in 1922. Together, they echo a widely accepted historical fact, which is the continuity of French Symbolist and Anglo-American Imagist poetry from the late nineteenth to the early twentieth century. The poems of Baudelaire and Eliot are masterpieces of the movement we call Modernism, and this book is about that movement, with Ezra Pound at the center of it as he was for more than half a century.

Many of the chapters that follow originated from papers given at various Ezra Pound International Conferences, in such far-flung places as Rapallo, Brantôme, Brunnenburg, Beijing, Paris, and Sun Valley. Looking back over them, I realized that there was a common theme running through them, which I have summarized in my title, *Ezra Pound and the Making of Modernism*. It gradually became clear to me as I studied his vast and complex work that Pound was the mastermind of Modernism, which is still the latest major intellectual and artistic movement in Western civilization. Modernism was a genuine Renaissance in arts and letters, as surely as the earlier Renaissance was. The first European Renaissance, of the fifteenth, sixteenth, and seventeenth centuries, moved from Italy northward to France and to England, inspiring such major artists and writers as Leonardo and Michelangelo and Ronsard and Shakespeare to create magnificent works of painting and sculpture and literature. The Modern Renaissance, of the nineteenth and twentieth centuries, originated in France and moved northwestward to England, Ireland, and the United States, inspiring works of painting, sculpture, music, dance, and literature, from the Impressionists to the Symbolists to the Imagists, from Monet and Rodin and Mallarmé and Debussy to Picasso and Stravinsky and Yeats and Joyce and Pound and Eliot and many more. Their individual achievements alone would have been impressive, but their many close friendships and their responses to the works they admired had a cumulative effect, producing new artistic and literary styles, the sum of which is Modernism. It was Pound who most of all promoted a new Renaissance, and it was he who had the critical discernment and creative imagination to be both a shaper of and a contributor to Modernism as a movement.

Though Modernism is no longer the active movement it once was, it is still the dominant force in arts and letters in the twenty-first century, because no comparable movement has as yet superseded or replaced it. Granted, there has been much talk about Postmodernism, but Postmodernism, so far as literature and the arts are concerned, is less a new movement than a reaction to Modernism. No matter what may be claimed for it, there are no major Postmodernist writers and works. What we have at the present moment of artistic and literary history are many competing theories and practices but no new and dominant movement. It is the right time to reappraise Modernism, and to assess the centrality to it of Ezra Pound's work. Such is the purpose of this book. Whether it is equal to the task is for future literary historians to judge.

INTRODUCTION:
EZRA POUND AND THE MAKING OF MODERNISM

"Athens was called the education of Hellas; from 1912 till 1922 Ezra Pound could have been called the education of poetry." So Randall Jarrell wrote in 1962 when he reviewed "Fifty Years of American Poetry." He looked back half a century and mused: "If in 1912 someone had predicted that during the next fifty years American poetry would be the best and most influential in the English language, and that the next generation of poets would establish once and for all the style and tone of American poetry, his prediction would have seemed fantastic. Yet all this is literally true of the generation of American poets that included Frost, Stevens, Eliot, Pound, Williams, Marianne Moore, Ransom."[1] Jarrell knew what he was talking about, since he was not only a gifted poet himself but *the* critic of the younger generation of Modern American poets. His was the second generation of poets in the new tradition, which emerged in the early twentieth century and changed the way poetry was written in English. By the time Jarrell wrote, Modernism was not simply American; it was international.

It had been international from the beginning, because its origins were not American. They were French, as Pound would have been the first to acknowledge. Modernism came out of two poetic movements, Realism and Symbolism, born simultaneously in France during the latter half of the nineteenth century. We think of Gustave Flaubert as the father of Realism, Charles Baudelaire as the father of Symbolism. Ezra Pound can be called the father of Modernism, since it was he more than any other writer who fused these two earlier literary movements. Like Flaubert and Baudelaire, Pound was a theorist as well as an artist, a critic as well as a poet. And though Flaubert and Baudelaire wrote in French in the nineteenth century, and

---

[1] Randall Jarrell, *The Third Book of Criticism* (New York: Farrar, Straus & Giroux, 1965) 295-96.

Pound wrote in English in the twentieth century, their work easily crossed linguistic boundaries, so that in time it was not only French and English literature but world literature that benefited from their potent combination of the creative and the critical.

It is difficult to reduce these three seminal literary movements to their essence. But what Flaubert sought above all was *le mot juste*, the exact word, grounded in his belief that a writer could tell the difference between words arbitrarily chosen and true verbal precision, between words that only approximated and words that matched reality. And what Baudelaire said he was trying to do was not only to write poems but to discover "the obscure laws" by which they came to be written; he wanted to find a rational way to account for something as irrational as poetic inspiration. Realism and Symbolism thus aimed at understanding literary art, not just producing it. Pound had the same aim, to make poetry embody what he called "permanent metaphor" and "absolute rhythm." The gist of his early essays was that metaphor and rhythm were not just arbitrary inventions ("cakeshop decorations," he sometimes called them), but fundamental, constitutive elements in the creation of poetry. "I believe in an 'absolute rhythm,'" he wrote early in his career, "a rhythm, that is, in poetry which corresponds exactly to the emotion or shade of emotion to be expressed."[2] In another early essay he spoke of "a like belief in a sort of permanent metaphor" which he said "is, as I understand it, 'symbolism' in its profounder sense."[3] Pound thus drew consciously from both French Realism and Symbolism when he championed Anglo-American Imagism, and in so doing initiated the revolutionary change of style that we call Modernism.

It is a century and a half since *Madame Bovary*, Flaubert's most famous novel, and *Les Fleurs du Mal*, Baudelaire's major collection of poems, were published in Paris in the same year, 1857. This year could be called Year One of Modernism, except that Modernism did not yet exist as a movement. These two books, both of which have become world

---

[2] Ezra Pound, "A Retrospect," 1918, in *Literary Essays of Ezra Pound,* ed.

T. S. Eliot (New York: New Directions, 1954) 9.

[3] Pound, "Vorticism," *Fortnightly Review*, XCVI, 1 (Sept. 1, 1914): 461-71.

classics, provoked such outrage from the reading public in France, of all places, that both authors were sued for public indecency and convicted. Such controversies are long since over, but Modernism still challenges us, and Pound is as controversial as ever. Modernism still challenges us, because two of its leading works, *The Waste Land* and *The Cantos*, have been exhaustively analyzed but not yet fully explained. And Pound, more than a quarter century after his death, is still controversial, partly because of his extraliterary activities, his outspoken Fascism and Antisemitism, but partly because his literary work still defies understanding, though it is more central to Modernism than ever. Pound, more than any single writer, set Modernism going in London in the second decade of the twentieth century. The beginning of Modernism does not have as definite a date as the beginnings of Realism and Symbolism, but the most likely year for its start is 1912, in London, when Pound published his seventh collection of poems, *Ripostes*. It was no accident that Pound chose a French title for a book of English poems, because he was in the habit of using French expressions freely in those days, and he took the word *riposte* or "counterthrust" from the sport of fencing, which he enjoyed practicing. When, fifty years later, Randall Jarrell looked back at 1912 as the birth-year of modern American poetry, he must have had Pound in mind. *Ripostes* was not Pound's first book of poems, but it was a departure from anything he had published before. It contained some new, very brief poems, associated with a new term, "Imagiste," and he boldly announced that "As for the future, *Les Imagistes* . . . have that in their keeping."

The claim turned out to be reasonably accurate. Pound was taking his cue from the French rather than the English, and deliberately choosing to follow the schools of Réalisme and Symbolisme with his new school of Imagisme. He first thought of "Les Imagistes" as a small group of English and American poets, but in 1914 he widened his net considerably. *Des Imagistes* was the title he gave the first Imagist anthology, still with the French spelling, though by then it was clear that this new movement was not French. It was Anglo-American, and included James Joyce and Ford Madox Ford, Richard Aldington and F. S. Flint, along with H. D., William Carlos Williams, Amy Lowell and Pound himself.

Imagism, the movement he launched in 1912, was the beginning of what came to be called Modernism. We have the authority of T. S. Eliot, who arrived in London too late to be part of the Imagist group, that "The *point de repère* usually and conveniently taken, as the starting point of modern poetry, is the group denominated 'imagist' in London about 1910."[4] Eliot was one of the first poets to learn from Pound, because even with a Harvard education he could see that Pound was ahead of him, and ahead of all the poets writing at that time. Pound knew how to educate other poets, because he had first educated himself.

He did so in two main stages: he began by studying "The Classics," not simply as the basis for various kinds of knowledge, but in order to know as much as he could about a specific kind of knowledge. What he studied from his earliest years was the finest poetry in a number of languages; and he then applied what he had learned about world poetry to the making of a new kind of poetry in English, experimenting with every known poetic form and encouraging other poets to do the same. It was Pound's firm principle that "No one language is complete," that "the artist should master all known forms and systems of metric," and so he began his ambitious program of self-education early in life, studying poetry and writing poems while he was still a schoolboy in Philadelphia. He was well on the way to his goal of knowing more about poetry than anyone living by the time he enrolled in college, starting with two years at the University of Pennsylvania in Philadelphia, then transferring for two years to Hamilton College in upstate New York, where he was freer to pursue his own course of study and earn a special Bachelor of Philosophy degree ("to avoid irrelevant subjects" he later said), where he could concentrate almost exclusively on language and literature. By the time he graduated from Hamilton in June of 1905, Pound had added, to his foundation in the Classical languages of Latin and Greek, which he had learned at school in Philadelphia, the Romance languages he had studied at Hamilton College in New York, including French, Spanish, Italian, Portuguese, and Provençal, as well as the Teutonic languages, German and Anglo-Saxon. After graduating from Hamilton, he went back to the University of Pennsylvania to do graduate work in Romance Philology,

---

[4] T. S. Eliot, "American Literature and the American Language," (first published in St. Louis in 1953, reprinted in *To Criticize the Critic* (New York: Farrar, Straus & Giroux, 1965) 58.

earned a Master's degree, and was on his way to earning a Doctor's degree by the time he left Penn in 1908. He paused for a brief period to teach French and Spanish at Wabash College in Indiana, before leaving under a cloud of scandal (this one involved a carnival girl he brought to his lodgings one night in Crawfordsville, but it set the pattern for Pound's whole controversial career) and moving abroad to Venice and London, where by 1912, Year One of Anglo-American Modernism, he had published seven books of poetry and one of prose. He never quite finished his doctoral degree, but he started a movement that revolutionized English poetry.

And so, by 1913, Pound could write a triumphant letter about what he had accomplished to Alice Corbin Henderson, assistant editor of *Poetry* magazine in Chicago. He wrote it from his flat at 10 Kensington Church Walk, London, the birthplace of Modernism. (It's worth mentioning that the building where he lived for five years now sports a Blue Plaque for Pound, placed there by the English Heritage Society, and officially unveiled in August, 2004, by Pound's daughter Mary.) His letter to Alice Corbin Henderson describes the kind of education he had insisted on giving himself by the age of 28:

> There simply is no one in America (or here either), who writes, and who has made anything like the study of the laws of the art, the fundamental eternal etc. in ten languages that I have. I set out 12 years ago, determined that whatever I might eventually be able to DO <compose>—(<creation> would depend on inspiration or any number of things outside my controll) this at least I could do and it would be my own fault and no one else's if I didn't. i.e. know more about poetry of every time and place. than any man living.[5]

Pound was boasting, but it was no empty boast, for he had conscientiously schooled himself in the world tradition of poetry in order to change its course. Modernism was born of his

---

[5] *The Letters of Ezra Pound to Alice Corbin Henderson*, ed. Ira Nadel

(Austin: University of Texas Press, 1993) 20.

dual program of poetic knowledge and creative experiment, a combination of theory and practice. Imagism as a movement was as much critical as creative, for Pound contributed "A Few Donts by an Imagiste" to *Poetry* magazine in 1913, at the very time when he was publishing new poems there. What was most revolutionary about Imagism was that it employed modern techniques to criticize modern life: its brief images were often ironic contrasts between past ages and the present age. More than any other writer, Pound knew what great poetry had been in the past and what it might be in the present, and he deliberately brought his knowledge of world poetry into touch with older poets as gifted as Yeats and Ford, and younger poets as gifted as Joyce and Eliot.

It was no wonder his fellow-poets were impressed by Pound's knowledge of world poetry and foreign languages, because it was encyclopedic. Even today, anyone who reads Pound is impressed by how much he knew, for no Pound expert, however well versed, could claim to equal him in sheer knowledge of poetry. We hold conferences that bring Pound scholars together, hoping that by pooling our knowledge we might approximate his. But though his learning was impressive, it was not superhuman. No reader needs to be intimidated by it, for Pound's learning had its limits: he did not fully *know* all the languages he read and translated from. I can recall a conversation I once had with his wife, Dorothy Shakespear Pound, in Washington in 1955, when I drove her to her basement flat near the grounds of St. Elizabeths, after both of us had sat at Ezra's feet all one afternoon, listening to him talk. I marveled aloud at his facility with languages, but she said it only went so far: she explained that Ezra believed in learning just enough of a language to understand its best poetry, so that he could translate it; that was all he was after. Pound drew much criticism from linguists who knew languages better than he did, a charge which was true. They pointed out mistakes in his translations that were sometimes glaring. His work with Chinese, especially, was attacked for what some called errors and others called "creative mistranslation," meaning that the poems in *Cathay* or in *The Classic Anthology as Defined by Confucius* were not literally accurate transcriptions of Chinese. They were good poems in English, but they were not word-for-word equivalents of the originals. These critics and detractors never bothered Pound, because he did not claim to know the languages better than they did; he had something else in mind. Dorothy Pound confided to me that while Ezra was working on his Confucian anthology in Washington, he often gave her Chinese ideograms to take down to the Library of Congress and gloss for him, since he didn't have the proper references handy at St. Elizabeths. Her insight into Pound's creative process showed that he knew his deficiencies, and did not hesitate to improve his knowledge of a language by whatever means necessary, no matter how cumbersome. He did not aim at complete knowledge of a foreign language; he aimed at knowing its best poetry, a knowledge as much intuitive as linguistic. To Pound, *how* a thing was said mattered as much as *what* was said. His kind of poetic knowledge was more practical than scholarly, because he wanted to translate poetry *as* poetry, to write original poems in English derived from poems in other languages. His best translations show how well he did it: they are of a variety and excellence unequalled so far as I know by any translator of poetry in the history of world literature.

To praise his translations is the same as to praise his poetry, because they are all of a piece. Think of "The Seafarer," for instance: is it a translation from the Anglo-Saxon or is it a poem in its own right? Many translators of Anglo-Saxon poetry have been influenced by that single translation since it first appeared in 1912; Seamus Heaney's celebrated recent translation of *Beowulf,* careful as it is, does not catch the swing of the four-beat alliterative Anglo-Saxon meter in Modern English as consistently as Pound did. Or take his Chinese translations: Eliot said that with *Cathay* Pound became "the inventor of Chinese poetry for our time." That was in 1915, and Pound's Chinese translations are still the best to be found in English, despite many errors, some conscious and some not. Eliot understood what Pound had done: rather than translate Chinese poetry literally into English, Pound wrote English poetry that was like Chinese poetry—like it, but not the same. Or think of his "Homage to Sextus Propertius," derived straight from Latin poetry, and deplored for its inaccuracies by Latin scholars as soon as it appeared in 1917. Thomas Hardy, however, appreciated what Pound had done, and told Pound he should have called it "Propertius Soliloquizes," since Pound had made it seem that the Latin poet of the Silver Age was writing modern poetry in English. Whatever Pound was, he was no ordinary translator. His enormously impressive knowledge of poetry in many languages was directed toward one end: making new poems of his own that pointed the way toward a new kind of English and American poetry.

Pound was what Stephen Spender called in *The Struggle of the Modern* a "revolutionary traditionalist." His understanding of Modernism was that it should be both radical and reactionary, realistic and symbolic, that what it owed to the past should be transformed into the present. Spender said that "The aims of the imagist movement in poetry provide the archetype of a modern creative procedure."[6] All Pound's translations were experiments in poetic form, moving from Anglo-Saxon alliterative rhythm to French *vers libre* to Greek and Latin hexameters to Italian sonnets to Chinese ideograms or verbal pictures. It was as much by his translations as by his original poems that Pound introduced formal variety into English, showing poets how to write with as many metrical variations as possible. All this metrical variety was meant to embody what he called "absolute rhythm," adapting the rhythm to the emotion of the poem, rather than adapting the emotion of the poem to fixed patterns of meter and rhyme, as had been the practice of most poets before him, much to their advantage. But Pound more than any poet "broke the heave of the pentameter" and his free verse was really free: his poetry was a set of poetic exercises, every poem in a different and unique form, even *The Cantos* chock full of metrical variety, whether the individual canto was long or short.

Free verse, or unlimited metrical variety, was one of the components of Imagism, and the other was what Pound called "permanent metaphor," concentrating imagery by understatement, by keeping words to a minimum. The Imagist rule, formulated by Pound, was "To use absolutely no word that does not contribute to the presentation"—an Imagist rule which Pound felt the later "Amygists" had violated. That the earlier Imagists had responded to his principle of verbal economy is illustrated by more than one anecdote. Richard Aldington said he once gave Pound a poem several lines long and asked him to examine it. Pound obliged, and when he returned the poem to Aldington, he had taken out all the words that did not contribute

---

[6] Stephen Spender, "The Seminal Image," in *The Struggle of the Modern* (Berkeley: U. of California, 1963) 110.

to the meaning. Aldington was amazed: there were only four words left! Pound even told such an anecdote about himself. He said that one evening when he got out of the Paris metro, he had an image in his head of the faces in a crowd, and he wrote a thirty-line poem to describe it. The poem didn't satisfy him, because he said it was "of second intensity," and so he reduced it to half the length, but he still wasn't satisfied, and then six months later he reduced it to two lines, thereby producing his most famous Imagist touchstone, "In a Station of the Metro":

> The apparition of these faces in the crowd:
> Petals on a wet, black bough.

His model in that case had not been French but Japanese; it was the *haiku*, traditionally only seventeen syllables long. Pound's influences were international. Not all Imagist poems were as short as that one, but it proved conclusively that Pound knew how to condense a poetic image to its essence, and he continued to condense his images and intensify their emotional force, even when he came to write longer poems, not in free verse but in rhyming quatrains, as he did when he produced *Hugh Selwyn Mauberley*, his ironic self-portrait, in 1920. His acknowledged metrical model in that case was French, the poems in Théophile Gautier's *Émaux et Camées*, but his images were as dense as ever, and his allusions from many languages intensified the texture of implied meanings. For instance, he introduced macaronic rhymes,

> Ιδμεν γαρ τοι πανθ' οσ ενι Τροιαε
> Caught in the unstopped ear
> Giving the rocks small leeway,
> The chopped seas held him therefore in that year.

where he played the sound of a long "a" in the Greek of Homer's *Odyssey*, the sound of Sirens singing to Ulysses "We know all you did in Troy," off against the same sound in English, written by his fictional poet, Mauberley, who was making a vain attempt to "maintain 'the sublime'" in poetry. Or again:

> Unaffected by 'the march of events,'
> He passed from men's memory in *l'an trentiesme*
> *de son eage;* The case presents
> No adjunct to the Muses' diadem.

Here he rhymed the English "diadem" with the medieval French *trentiesme* of Villon's *Grand Testament*, where "in the thirtieth year of his age" Mauberley is about to leave the civilized world for the South Seas, as Pound's fictional Mauberley did after his unsuccessful endeavor to achieve poetic immortality in London. Allusions in two foreign languages enrich the already concentrated imagery of the poem, and quoting them in the original was Pound's way of using his extensive knowledge of poetry in ancient and medieval languages to add complexity to his own poetry. Modernism, in Pound's hands, was never static: it evolved from brief Imagist poems in free verse into long allusive and ironic poems in meter and rhyme, and then into even longer poems in *The Cantos*.

Perhaps the most astonishing feat Pound ever accomplished in his effort to condense images by taking out all the unnecessary words was his editing of *The Waste Land*. We can't examine the longer text of Aldington's poem, which Pound reduced to four words, because it no longer exists, nor can we look at the original thirty lines of Pound's Metro poem, which he distilled into two lines, but we can examine the full text of what Eliot called his "sprawling, chaotic poem," which he carried to Paris from Switzerland in 1921, hoping Pound could help him make sense of it. Pound helped him so much that the result was the central masterpiece of Modern Poetry, a poem written by Eliot and edited by Pound. Pound didn't write the poem but he helped Eliot perfect it, and Eliot said the poem was printed just as it was when it left Pound's hand. Eliot thought the manuscript would offer conclusive proof of the value of Pound's editorial work if it were found, but he died thinking it was lost. It wasn't lost; Eliot had made a present of it to his chief patron, the American lawyer John Quinn, who died in 1924, two years after the poem was published. Quinn passed it on to his wife, who passed it on to their daughter, and it was eventually sold by Quinn's daughter to the New York Public Library, where it was discovered in 1968, three years after Eliot's death. Eliot's widow Valerie edited and published a facsimile of the manuscript fifty years after the poem was published. Here we can see exactly what Pound left out, which amounted to nearly half the lines Eliot had written. What he left in it was the poem Eliot published in 1922, transformed by Pound's careful editing into a SuperImagist poem. *The Waste Land* as we know it is a tightly condensed series of allusive and ironic images that are familiar to every reader today, because they appear in every respectable anthology of English poetry.

Pound knew exactly what Eliot had achieved in *The Waste Land*, and no sooner had he finished editing it than he hailed it as "the justification of the 'movement,' of our modern experiment, since 1900."[7] He thought Eliot had done for poetry what Joyce had done for the novel with *Ulysses*, which by a remarkable coincidence was published the same year as Eliot's epochmaking poem. In Pound's view, Joyce and Eliot had modernized literature in English, much as Flaubert and Baudelaire had done earlier in French literature. Modernism had been fully justified in the decade from 1912 to 1922, and though it continued to be the main literary movement through the remainder of the twentieth century, its highest achievement was the poem Eliot wrote and Pound edited. *The Waste Land* still stands as the most revolutionary Modern poem, and it is an example of the sort of "permanent metaphor" and "absolute rhythm" which Pound advocated and practiced, and from which many other poets learned. It was the culmination of a decade of experiment with form and imagery that had been promoted by Pound and completed by Eliot.

What came after *The Waste Land* in the history of Modernism was a century of new poetry, much of it good, some of it great, and particularly in Pound's case, *The Cantos*. Pound had begun this long series of poems, his lifework, before 1922, but he lived another fifty years and wrote and translated poetry the rest of his life, just as he had done earlier. He might have learned from editing Eliot's long poem how to edit his own longer poems, but unfortunately he did not seem to apply the Imagist rules as carefully to his own later work as he did to Eliot's. If he had done so, *The Cantos* would be half as long as they are, and most of his readers would probably agree they would be better. *The Cantos*, for all their brilliance, are too

---

[7] *The Letters of Ezra Pound, 1907-1941*, ed. D. D. Paige (New York: Harcourt, Brace, 1950) 180.

wordy at times, in contradiction of Pound's Imagist principles, yet they represent the full range of Pound's extraordinary knowledge of world poetry, which is evident in every Canto, especially those Cantos in which the strange calligraphic Chinese language is either quoted, translated, or paraphrased. Pound learned Western languages from his teachers at the University of Pennsylvania and Hamilton College, but he taught himself Chinese. He did so in London with the help of Ernest Fenollosa's notes, and he mastered this highly complex language so well he not only produced *Cathay*, clearly one of his masterpieces, but translated a number of Japanese Noh plays, and all of the Chinese works attributed to Confucius, the prose as well as the poetry. He also used Chinese extensively in *The Cantos*, sometimes with excellent results, as in *Canto XIII*, a creditable *persona* of Confucius, the ancient Chinese philosopher, and in *Canto XLIX*, the "Seven Lakes Canto," an Imagist sequence based on some Chinese paintings he had been shown in Rapallo. Sometimes, however, as in the long series on Chinese history, *Cantos LII* to *LXI*, his reliance on Chinese exposed the shortcomings of his self-education. These middle cantos read too much like potted history, full of names and dates, surely the most boring section of the whole poem. But in *The Pisan Cantos* and other late cantos, the Chinese characters provide visual as well as verbal variety, and Pound often translates them into English for readers who do not know Chinese.

Overall, it was Pound's education in world poetry which helped make Modernism what it was, the latest major movement in Western literature. *The Cantos* were almost complete when Randall Jarrell surveyed fifty years of American poetry in 1952, and he called them "less a 'poem containing history' [one of Pound's descriptions] than a heap containing poetry, history, recollections, free associations, obsessions."[8] If they are a heap, they are a fertile heap, a compost pile made up of scraps and pieces of Pound's electrifying personality and his wide-ranging fund of knowledge and experience. The only form Pound claimed for them was that of the Ideogram, a mosaic of images derived from his reading of Chinese characters. He never completed them, but his 117 cantos come in a variety of shapes and lengths and show that Modernism went on

---

[8] Jarrell, *Third Book of Criticism*, 304.

developing in Pound's work, both in the theoretical and practical sense, because his constant metrical invention never flagged (Pound's work as a whole has more rhythmical variety than that of any major poet), and his images were freshly illuminating and arresting.

> Like a fish-scale roof
> Like the church roof in Poictiers
> *Canto IV*

The enormous tragedy of the dream in the peasant's bent shoulders
> *Canto LXXIV*

> A little light, like a rushlight
> To lead back to splendour
> *Canto CXVI*

It is no wonder that Pound's work has been a source-book for other poets. *The Cantos* at their best remain an inexhaustible fund of poetic ingenuity and skill, and he could not have written them if he had not made good on his boast to Alice Corbin Henderson in 1913, that he knew more about poetry than any living man. Pound's Modernism as it evolved was both a reflection and a critique of the age he lived in; if he had been any less embroiled in its politics and economics, he would have been less controversial, but he would also have been less representative of his age. His inexhaustible metrical variety came straight from his original belief in "absolute rhythm," and his densely allusive, ironic images bore out his similar belief in "permanent metaphor." Knowing as much as he did about world poetry, in a number of different languages past and present, and having the ambition and the talent to write great poetry himself, he started a revolution in English literary style that continued through the twentieth century, not just in his own work but in the work of other poets. Pound joked that editing Eliot's *Waste Land* was like performing a Caesarean Operation. So it was, and by it he became not only the Father, but the Midwife, of Modernism. He had presided over its birth, its maturity, even its old age, outliving all three of his most brilliant contemporaries, Yeats, Joyce, and Eliot. Ezra Pound was as Randall Jarrell later said "the education of poetry." His influence extended far beyond the poets he knew in London when Modernism was born. Indeed, Pound is still educating every reader of his poetry, because his work as a whole, early and late, challenges us to understand him in order to understand our age—ultimately, that is, to understand ourselves.

POUND'S MUTATION: TRANSLATING SYMBOLISM INTO IMAGISM

T. S. Eliot, writing about Ezra Pound in 1946, at the low point of his fortunes, when few had anything good to say about him, credited him with bringing about an "abrupt mutation of poetic form,"[1] that is, with nothing less than the creation of a new poetic style in English. Eliot's words acknowledged his own personal debt to Pound and at the same time recognized Pound's exceptional originality. More than half a century has passed since Eliot wrote those words, but the singular contribution of Pound to Modern Poetry is increasingly recognized, and Pound has acquired a reputation that rivals that of Edgar Allan Poe, an equally eccentric American poet who was so original that he created new genres as well as new works. We think of Poe as the inventor of the detective story, the Gothic romance, the prose poem, and even, some would say, the Symbolist poem, while Pound's chief invention was a new poetic style which he christened Imagism, which became the essential twentieth century literary style in English, not only in poetry but in prose. Imagist style—dense, concrete, understated, ironic and ambiguous—can be identified with the poetic style of Eliot and the prose style of Hemingway, the signature styles of twentieth-century American literature So Pound's achievement can be measured not only by the works he created on his own but by what he did for others: he recognized Eliot's poetic talent in London before anyone else did, got his first poems published, and insisted that he become a poet rather than a philosopher; and Hemingway has testified in *A Moveable Feast* that he learned much about how to write from Pound in Paris in the 1920s.

Pound and Poe are an unlikely pair, but both were regarded in their time as mad geniuses. Poe was an alcoholic, a gambler, a dropout from the army and the university, whose behavior disgraced his adoptive father and almost everyone who

---

[1] T. S. Eliot, "Ezra Pound (1946)" in *A Collection of Essays to be Presented to Ezra Pound on His 65th Birthday*, ed. Peter Russell (London: Peter Nevill, 1950) 30.

knew him, whereas Pound brought shame on himself by his political and economic obsessions, especially when expressed publicly through wartime radio broadcasts against his own country. Pound lived longer and was vilified more thoroughly than Poe, for he was imprisoned by his own countrymen in Italy, flown as a prisoner to the United States, indicted for treason, judged incompetent to stand trial, and finally incarcerated for thirteen years in an insane asylum in Washington. That was when Eliot wrote his tribute. But today, Poe's sins have been largely forgiven, and he is known for his great originality and his crucial role in literary history. Pound is still controversial—an advantage in the short run, since it has kept public attention on a great poet after his death—but in the long run the controversies are bound to fade and Pound's place in literary history will seem as indispensable as Poe's, for as Eliot also said, Pound was the writer mainly responsible for the twentieth century revolution in poetry.

Pound was an innovator himself, and he helped others to follow. One of the most innovative was e. e. cummings, a poet so original he was credited by the critic Lionel Trilling with liberating even the parts of speech. For Cummings, Pound was "the authentic 'innovator,' the true trailblazer of an epoch."[2] And that was not all: as a great translator of poetry, Pound managed the unprecedented feat of translating one new poetic style into another, for it was chiefly in his hands that French Symbolism became Anglo-American Imagism. The debt all English-language poets owed to Pound was summed up by Donald Davie, an admirer but not a disciple of Pound, who wrote, late in the twentieth century, that "certain French poets of the last century have a better title than anyone else to be thought the fathers of Anglo-American modernism in poetry."[3]

Pound like Poe was a theorist as well as a poet, or as Baudelaire said of Poe, he was "both a scholar and an artist." The same was true of Baudelaire himself, and of other leading French Symbolists who like Baudelaire translated the works of Poe into excellent French, notably Mallarmé and Valéry. The

---

[2] Quoted by Humphrey Carpenter in *A Serious Character: The Life of Ezra Pound* (Boston: Houghton Mifflin, 1988) 402.

[3] Donald Davie, *Two Ways Out of Whitman*, ed. Doreen Davie (Manchester: Carcanet, 2000) 196.

potent combination of original critical theory and new poetic experiment made Symbolism the most influential poetic movement of the late nineteenth century; it was a similar combination of theory and practice that made Imagism the most influential poetic movement of the early twentieth century. Great poetic movements are even rarer than great poets, but both the French Symbolists and the Anglo-American Imagists had what was needed to make a lasting impact: exceptional poetic talent combined with a profound understanding of the creative process. The talents were individual; the poetic theories were universal.

The chief source of knowledge about the close relation between the French Symbolists and the American Imagists is a book written for a doctorate at the Sorbonne in 1929. The author was Réné Taupin; he called it *L'Influence du Symbolisme Français sur la Poésie Américaine, de 1910 à 1920*[4] (my wife and I translated it into English, with Taupin's approval, as *The Influence of French Symbolism on Modern American Poetry*[5]). Taupin's study focused on the Imagist Decade, the second decade of the twentieth century, when Modern Poetry in English emerged out of the turbulent period during which the First World War was fought in Europe. Taupin provided what is still the best overview of Pound's extraordinary feat, which was nothing less than the transformation of one poetic movement into another, Symbolism in French into Imagism in English, a fruitful coupling of the two most original and broadly in-fluential movements in modern literature.

Before examining what Taupin learned about the relation between these two movements, perhaps we should start with working definitions of the terms "Symbolism" and "Imag-ism," since after a hundred years of frequent use they continue to be elusive. Many have tried to define them, but so far no single definition of either term has prevailed. It is best to start with what a leading Symbolist poet and a leading Imagist poet had to say. Stéphane Mallarmé wrote memorably that "The ideal is to *suggest* the object. It is the perfect use of this mystery

---

[4] Paris: Henri Champion, 1928.

[5] New York: AMS Press, 1985.

which constitutes the symbol."[6] And Ezra Pound wrote, just as memorably, "An 'Image' is that which presents an intellectual and emotional complex in an instant of time."[7] If we compare these two definitions, by the poets most responsible for inventing the terms, we can say that Symbolism was a suggestive art of indirect expression, while Imagism was an objective art of direct presentation. To put it another way, Symbolism used words to create a prolonged and heightened state of consciousness, while Imagism used words to create an instant of intensified consciousness. Symbolism, it might be said, is a technique for expanding consciousness to include perceptions hitherto unexpressed, while Imagism is a technique for integrating consciousness by investing a moment of time with universal import. The two movements appear to offer opposite theories for creating poems. But they do have some-thing in common, for Symbolism, by teasing out the meanings implied in words, forces the reader to participate in the imaginative act of the poet, thus sustaining the effect of heightened consciousness, while Imagism, by its strict economy of words, demands that the reader call up an image from his own mind, perceiving for himself what a moment of intense consciousness may contain. However we define Symbolism and Imagism, there is in them a striking difference in poetic technique linked to a surprising likeness in reader psychology.

T. E. Hulme, the British philosopher and poet who learned about "Creative Evolution" from Henri Bergson at the Sorbonne, presided over the original School of Images in 1908-10 in London, and was the first to stress the crucial importance of the poetic image. In one of his few but highly illuminating lectures, Hulme spoke approvingly of "The new art of the Reader: Sympathy with the reader as brother, as unexpressed author."[8] Readers of Baudelaire may hear an echo of À Lecteur, the opening poem of *Les Fleurs du Mal*, the first book of truly modern poems, in those words of Hulme:

---

[6] Quoted in *Modernisms: A Literary Guide* by Peter Nicholls (Berkeley: U. of California, 1995) 36.

[7] Ezra Pound, "A Retrospect," 4.

[8] T. E. Hulme, "Notes on Language and Style," in *Further Speculations*, ed. Sam Hynes (Minneapolis: U. of Minnesota, 1955) 93.

—Hypocrite lecteur,—mon semblable,—mon frère!

So if the Symbolists and the Imagists had different techniques for writing poems, they started with a similar impulse to engage their readers in the poem by deliberate ambiguity, thus drawing the reader into the poem to interpret it. Both movements sought to challenge readers intellectually, a challenge that, it must be admitted, not all readers have welcomed, and so Symbolist poetry like Imagist poetry has often seemed too difficult for many readers to grasp. But both Mallarmé and Pound clearly wanted to startle the reader into a creative attitude, to force his imagination to work, and they did so by provocative new uses of language. Pound insisted that Imagism was not Symbolism, yet, as F. S. Flint wrote in his "History of Imagism" which was published in the *Egoist* magazine in 1915, it was Pound who "invented the term 'Imagisme' to designate the aesthetic of 'Les Imagistes,'" and by using French spellings for his invented terms, as well as by calling his first anthology *Des Imagistes*, Pound, despite his disclaimer, clearly wanted Imagism to have much in common with Symbolism.

Taupin, in his exhaustive study of Symbolism and Imagism, built on the definitions given by Mallarmé and Pound and provided his own more expansive definitions. He explained that "Symbolism was based on the principle of suggestion," that "Suggestion was based on the psychology of the association of ideas," and that "The resultant pleasure of such poetry is the atmosphere of dream brought on by the indefinite suggestivity of symbols." He contrasted the Symbolist effect in poetry with the Imagist effect by saying that "The Imagists never painted; they always named, and directly; and the pleasure of their poetry is not the satisfaction of discovering little by little, but of seizing at a single blow, in the fullest vitality, the image, a fusion of reality in words."[9] Taupin saw that there were obvious differences of technique in the two movements, since the suggestive association of implied meanings was the Symbolist method of using words, while the direct verbal description of an object to form a mental image was the Imagist method. "The Imagists did not suggest; they evoked immediately," he

---

[9] Taupin, *The Influence of French Symbolism on Modern American Poetry*, translated by Anne Rich Pratt and William Pratt, 96.

observed, while the Symbolists strove to create a mood or atmosphere surrounding the subject. But since in both cases the resulting poem forced the reader to think hard about what the subject was, whether it was real or a dream, and to picture it in his own imagination, Taupin felt justified in concluding that "Between the 'image' of the Imagists and the 'symbol' of the Symbolists there is a difference only of precision."[10] Thus, the intended subject of a poem might be either a "symbol" or an "image," challenging the reader to divine the meaning, but the poetic form should be elastic enough to contain it, and the French Symbolists developed what they called *vers libre* as a more flexible verse form than meter or rhyme. It was taken over literally by the Imagists as "free verse" in their experiments, following Pound's famous pronouncement that became one of the three cardinal rules of Imagism: "As regarding rhythm: to compose in the sequence of the musical phrase, not in sequence of a metronome." In Taupin's view, "Pound introduced a new music into English," having discovered that the intricate metrical variations he found in his early study of the Greek Classical poets and the French troubadours led to the sort of experiments with poetic form that the contemporary French Symbolists were making. What is most surprising in Taupin's treatment of this new poetic form is that he thought it was dependent on the difference, not so much between Symbolism and Imagism, as between the French and English languages. He argued that:

> In English, the question of syllable count is less important than in French, for English words are not so easily measured as are French words, every syllable of which is pronounced with a nearly equal value. That is why free verse is perhaps more logical in English than in French, since syllabication is less strict. [11]

It is certainly true that "free verse" was a more revolutionary technique in English than in French, for it led to a radical change in the writing of poetry, and it may be that it was more

---

[10] Taupin, 93.

[11] Taupin, 109.

logical as well, for poets in English quickly tended to adopt the greater informality of free verse and to shun the formality of meter and rhyme, a departure in technique which was more conspicuous in English than in French. Of course, having established the possibility of free verse in English, Pound came to view it as too loose in practice, hence his imitation of the formal meter and rhyme of Gautier's *Émaux et Camées (Enamels and Cameos)* when he came to compose his long post-Imagist sequence, *Hugh Selwyn Mauberley.* But free verse is the primary poetic form in *The Cantos,* and so Pound's Imagist experiments were never really abandoned, just temporarily suspended for the sake of variety.

If French Symbolism differed from Anglo-American Imagism both in its use of verbal music and in its treatment of the subject, Pound knew he was working from a model that had renewed the art of poetry in the French language and he believed it could be used to renew the art of poetry in the English language. What Taupin calls "The Imagist Attack" used French Symbolism as a weapon against English Victorianism and used it effectively. He argued that "Perhaps it could be said that Imagism gave America an artistic tradition which the sterile and facile imitation of England had long prevented."[12] There is no doubt that the very foreignness of French poetry appealed to Pound, and that was why he insisted on the French spelling of the words Imagisme and Imagistes, to emphasize that this was a movement outside the strictly English poetic tradition. Once he had succeeded, and succeeded so well that, as Taupin wryly put it, "American poetry spoke French," there was no longer a need for an Imagist movement, because by the end of the Imagist decade, poets like T. S. Eliot were ready to reassert the English tradition by means of the poetry of the Metaphysicals, such as Donne and Marvell and even Shakespeare. There was now room to reassess the English poetic tradition from a new vantage point, for as Taupin concludes in what still seems the definitive study of the two movements: "In the English language, it was the Imagists, led by Pound and following the example of the French Symbolists, who stripped poetry of

---

[12] Taupin, 217.

sentiment and ornament, and renewed the poetic potentialities of the language." [13]

Taupin's firm principle throughout his study was that "True influence consists in surpassing one's model, not in reproducing it."[14] And, in the course of his study, he cited a number of instances of the deliberate imitation by American poets of French poets, producing a too obvious kind of American Symbolist poetry that had little lasting effect. He contrasted these abortive attempts at starting an American Symbolist movement by imitation with Pound's invention of a new movement which he dubbed Imagism, based on real influence, where the effect was permanent. Pound provided Taupin with his most telling example of the successful use of a French Symbolist model for an American Imagist poem: his transformation of a rather obscure work, Henri de Régnier's title poem in *Médailles d'Argile (Medallions of Clay)*, into the celebrated poem, "The Return," often anthologized after its first appearance in *Ripostes* in 1912. Not only did Pound greatly condense the French original when he wrote his English poem, but he changed its main image from a clay medallion to something like a silverpoint etching, keeping in his poem only the subject, the reappearance of gods to men, and the free verse counterpoint of the French model. The proof that Pound's poem surpassed its model is that it is much better known today than de Régnier's poem. "Medailles d'Argile" by a minor Symbolist poet is part of the history of French literature, but "The Return" is one of the best-known works of a major American poet. Though "The Return" is still puzzling to most readers, it is widely anthologized, and so it has come to be a model of Imagist poetics. De Régnier's original French poem is more dreamlike in its approach to the subject, the imagined return of pagan gods, whereas Pound's poem has the effect of making the vision seem real, and thus it could be said that Pound objectified the dream which de Régnier projected. Pound's poem is much briefer, much more dramatic, and also more ambiguous. Yeats liked the poem so much that he placed it at the end of "A Packet for Ezra Pound" which he wrote as a preface for the revised edition of his most complex prose work, *A Vision*, and the

---

[13] Taupin, 250-51.

[14] Taupin, 171.

context he provided for it gave the poem new meaning, as the prelude to a wide-ranging overview of Yeats's own visionary poems—hardly what Pound had in mind when he composed it. But as Symbolism presents us with poems that unfold in the mind of the reader, so Imagism presents us with poems that acquire meaning with interpretation. Pound's poem is a new work derived from another work in another language, but its meaning is not dependent on the original model; rather, it is dependent upon what readers of English make of it—including a fellow poet like Yeats if he so chose. It is not necessary to know that Pound got his inspiration from a French Symbolist poem, but if we do know it, we can more fully appreciate his mastery of the translator's art, and also how much he accomplished by his feat of changing Symbolism into Imagism.

Admittedly, Pound's poem is only one exceptional instance of the influence of French Symbolism on Modern American Poetry, but it was enough for Taupin to prove his point, for most of his study tends to prove the contrary, that it is rare when true influence occurs, that is, when the model is surpassed by the work it inspires. He cites only one other such instance, this time of a poem by Eliot, "Rhapsody on a Windy Night," based on a poem by Jules Laforgue, "Complainte de Cette Bonne Lune" ("Complaint of This Good Moon"). Taupin definitely did regard Eliot as an Imagist, who carried the movement to a "second stage" in which the advances in English poetry Pound had initiated were further explored and consolidated. Eliot's poem contains an actual quotation—or rather, a deliberate misquotation—in French, which gives the influence away but does not, Taupin thinks, diminish it. Eliot admitted that he was much influenced by Laforgue in his early poetry, long before he met Pound, and in "Rhapsody on A Windy Night" he adapted one of his lines:

> *La lune ne garde aucune rancune*
> ("The moon bears no grudge")

from Laforgue's "Complainte de Cette Bonne Lune," a close paraphrase of the French poet's line:

> *la Lune/Ne gardons pas ainsi rancune*
> ("we don't bear the moon any grudge").

Eliot's use of the line, however, placed a few words of French inside a much longer poem in English, the whole of which was not about the moon but about the speaker's nightmarish journey through a hostile city. Like Pound's "The Return," Eliot's "Rhapsody on a Windy Night" has become better known than Laforgue's poem, and thus Taupin is justified in speaking of it as he speaks of Pound's debt to de Régnier—a case of true influence, where the new poem surpasses its model.

Taupin does not mention other close analogies between Symbolism and Imagism in his study, since he completed it in 1929, but a reader today could easily find further parallels, whether they are the result of influence or not, between Symbolist and Imagist poems. For instance, Taupin does not mention a pair of Symbolist and Imagist poems that are strikingly alike: Verlaine's "Art Poétique" and MacLeish's "Ars Poetica." "Art Poétique" is French, the work of Paul Verlaine, who is usually thought of as the most musical of the Symbolists, and "Ars Poetica" is American, written by Archibald MacLeish, a poet too young to participate in the Imagist movement from its beginning, but one who clearly benefited from Pound's poetic mutation, his translation of Symbolism into Imagism. Not only do the poems have similar titles, but Verlaine's "Art Poétique" and MacLeish's "Ars Poetica" can be said to embody in poetic form the main theories of Symbolism and Imagism.

The two poems read as follows in English (my translation):

"The Art of Poetry"

By Paul Verlaine

Music is first, above all else,
So give it an uneven line,
varied, soluble in air,
floating lightly, supple, fine.

Remember, you should never choose
your words without an overtone;
nothing's better than a song
where vagueness and precision join.

Behold bright eyes behind a veil,
a clear day shimmering at noon,
or, in a chilly autumn sky
dazzling stars around the moon!

Nuance is what we truly seek—
not Color—for Nuance alone
has the subtlety to wed
dream to dream and flute to horn!

Flee from pointed Epigrams,
obscene Laughter, jabbing Wit,
enough to make the heavens weep,
too much garlic in the pot!

Take eloquence and wring its neck!
And while you're at it, you'll be well
advised to check the rule of Rhyme,
for what it does no one can tell.

Oh, to catalogue the wrongs
that Rhyme has done—what slave or child
would be beguiled by this cheap gem
so false, so hollow, so defiled?

Music, Music, evermore!
Let your verse take wings and fly,
soaring like a soul that seeks
another love, another Sky.

Make your verse a lucky charm,
crisp as a morning wind is, pure
as the scents of mint or thyme...
all the rest is literature.

"Ars Poetica"

By Archibald MacLeish

A poem should be palpable and mute
As a globed fruit

Dumb
As old medallions to the thumb

Silent as the sleeve-worn stone
Of casement ledges where the moss has grown—

A poem should be wordless
As the flight of birds

A poem should be motionless in time
As the moon climbs

Leaving, as the moon releases
Twig by twig the night-entangled trees,

Leaving, as the moon behind the winter leaves,
Memory by memory the mind—

A poem should be motionless in time
As the moon climbs

A poem should be equal to:
Not true

For all the history of grief
An empty doorway and a maple leaf

For love
The leaning grasses and two lights above the sea—

A poem should not mean
But be.

Verlaine's poem, written in the 1880s when the Symbolist movement was just emerging in French poetry, starts by emphasizing Music, which to Verlaine was the primary poetic technique, and to him unrhymed verse was the most musical poetic form. Verlaine is thus arguing poetically for free verse; however, he chose to write his definitive Symbolist poem in quatrains with end rhymes. It is one of the paradoxes of the

French Symbolists that they invented *vers libre* but used it sparingly—more sparingly than the Imagists, in fact, which tends to prove Taupin's point that free verse is more natural in English than in French. Verlaine's poem denounces regularity of rhythm and rhyme, along with conventional metaphors, calling instead for "bright eyes behind a veil" and "dazzling stars around the moon," a poetic way of saying that metaphors must be unconventional and unpredictable. Similarly, he favors "Nuance" over "Color," because it is a more subtle visual effect, thus more difficult to create. And at the end of "The Art of Poetry," Verlaine urges breezily that a poem should be light-hearted, a "lucky charm," seeming "as crisp as a morning wind, as pure / as the scent of mint or thyme"—fresh metaphors for the new freedom which the poet is trying to evoke with his words. In short, Verlaine wants to move the Art of Poetry away from the older, traditional "literature," which he scorns, into a new form, freeing the imagination by subtle shades of meaning and symbolic overtones, allowing the poem to fly like "a soaring soul" to imagined worlds beyond the earthbound world of the senses.

MacLeish's poem, in contrast, takes the form of a series of terse free verse couplets with occasional rhymes, demonstrating that the Imagists were willing to go much further than the Symbolists with free verse, making it into a standard English technique, the normal poetic form of the twentieth century. In defining what a poem should be, instead of dealing with abstract ideas like "Music" and "Nuance" and "soul" and "literature," MacLeish sets forth a poetic theory in a succession of brief, concrete, paradoxical images. He says a poem should be "palpable and mute" like "globed fruit" and "dumb as old medallions to the thumb," "silent as the sleeve-worn stone" and "wordless as a flight of birds"—as if a poem could ever be a speechless and solid part of the real world, rather than a construct of symbolic words. Each image is complete in itself, intended to be the equivalent of a poem, and the combined effect is to make the poem seem an object, not an idea, which in the final paradox "should not mean but be." Readers have puzzled especially over the final two lines of this poem, which seem self-contradictory, yet which effectively convey the sense that poems can exist beyond the meanings of the words they contain, that there is a permanence in poetic expression that lasts through time. MacLeish's title is Latin, not French, and is borrowed from a treatise by Horace, not from a French Symbolist poet, yet it is a legitimate offspring of Verlaine's poem. MacLeish's Imagist definition of poetry seems to point to brevity and concreteness as the qualities that are most enduring, and to demonstrate by its very form that free verse with occasional rhymes is preferable to regular meter and rhyme. MacLeish's "Ars Poetica" was written in the 1920s, a decade after Pound had launched the Imagist movement, but it seems to bear out Pound's earlier belief that "It is better to create one Image in a lifetime than to produce voluminous works."[14]

Verlaine, the Symbolist par excellence, wanted poetry to be subtle and elusive, while MacLeish, the Imagist counterpart, wanted poetry to be concrete and brief. One may wonder what, finally, Symbolism and Imagism have in common. The answer is that both are designed to make the reader think as well as feel; they appeal as much to the mind as to the senses; they induce a state of consciousness in which the reader is aware that poetry stimulates ordinary words to produce extraordinary meanings. "An 'Image' is an intellectual and emotional complex in an instant of time," Pound said. Pound knew that the French Symbolists had revivified the French language in order to create new poems, and he thought he could use their example to revitalize the English language in order to create new poetry. He did so, and Imagism was born out of Symbolism. It was no simple imitative process but a complex translation of poetic theories and practices from one language to another. Verlaine's poem and MacLeish's poem do not look alike, even though they have almost identical titles, yet each is an example of the poetic art which each is defining. Pound's original intuition was right: as Symbolist poetry enriched the French language, so Imagist poetry enriched the English language. The movements were complementary, and new possibilities for poetic expression were created in each language. Pound achieved what Eliot called the "mutation" of a new poetic style in English by grafting new poems in one language onto the root stock of an earlier poetic style in another language. The two movements produced different poems on the same subject, defining poetically what makes a good poem—whether by following the Symbolist principles of Verlaine's "The Art of Poetry," or the Imagist principles of MacLeish's "Ars Poetica." These two poems are as different as the movements out of which they came, and yet they are also alike, since each is trying to define the mystery of poetry, a reality beyond the words of the poem, as Taupin well understood when he came to the conclusion that "Between the 'image' of the Imagists and the 'symbol' of the Symbolists there is a difference only of precision."

2

POUND'S POETIC TRANSFORMATIONS

When Pound published *The Pisan Cantos* in 1948, he could reasonably claim: "To have gathered from the air a live tradition / Or from a fine old eye the unconquered flame / This is not vanity." Clearly, it was not vanity, for Pound had engineered nothing less than a revolution in English poetic style in the twentieth century. His main means of doing so was a departure from tradition, however, because he did it by openly borrowing from other poets, a practice he had adopted from his earliest poetic experiments. He became so gifted at appropriating the work of other poets that T. S. Eliot would acknowledge, looking back in 1954, that "Mr. Pound is more responsible for the XXth Century revolution in poetry than is any other individual."[1]

Among Pound's very early poems, at least two show how willing he was to borrow from other poets, to take his inspiration directly from reading poetry of earlier periods in English, or by drawing on his wide acquaintance with ancient and modern languages. The first is "The Tree" and the second is "Histrion." In "The Tree," he extracts the myths of Apollo and Daphne and Baucis and Philemon from Greek literature and puts them into English, thereby transforming himself into sacred laurel and oak trees in order to know the secrets of nature, "the truth of things unseen before." Here, in what was perhaps Pound's earliest original poem of real distinction, he drew on Greek mythology, but he did not simply translate or imitate it. "The Tree" is in fact one of his Hilda poems, written for the poet he later named H. D., his "Dryad," or "wood nymph." He imagined undergoing a dual metamorphosis, for he begins the poem, "I stood still and was a tree amid the wood," and goes on to appropriate the Apollo and Daphne myth, in which the woman alone (that would be H. D.) is transformed into a laurel tree, and then the Baucis and Philemon myth, in which both the man and the woman (that would be himself and H. D.) are reincarnated as oak trees.

---

[1] Eliot, "Introduction" to *Literary Essays of Ezra Pound* (New York: New Directions, 1954) xi.

Having used Greek myths to transform himself into nature in "The Tree," Pound in "Histrion" deliberately sets out to transform himself into real poets he has read. He mentions Dante and François Villon as the poets he admires most and wishes to emulate. But he places them, quite surprisingly, in the company of religious figures, not poets. These were also heroes of his youth, when, as is often forgotten, Pound was a confirmed Presbyterian who read the Bible daily. When he speaks of "Christus and John and eke the Florentine," he is equating Christ and John the Baptist with Dante and Villon as inspirations for poetry. And indeed, unlikely as it may seem now, Christ was probably Pound's first successful poetic reincarnation, since "The Ballad of the Goodly Fere" brought him to serious attention among readers early in the twentieth century, when it was printed in an anthology of Victorian poetry, while his last successful poetic reincarnation was undoubtedly that of Dante in *The Cantos*, when he had become the most avant garde of Modern Poets. Pound's capacity for imaginative metempsychosis was realized in both the early and the later poems, for Pound was never content to translate or imitate alone; he wanted to bring the dead back to life, chiefly the poets he admired the most, to make them live again in the present and speak to the readers of his time as they had spoken first to him. He could even joke sometimes about his extravagant ambition to clothe the dead in modern dress, as he did in an early burlesque called "Redondillas, or Something of That Sort":

I am really quite modern, you know,
despite my affecting the ancients.[2]

He might mock his penchant for role-playing, but he was clearly serious about his major ambition of reincarnating past heroes. He would later choose to start his "forty-year epic," *The Cantos*, by impersonating Ulysses and going, not with him but *as* him, on a journey to Hell to speak with the dead.

Surely no poet, including Eliot, ever borrowed from as many poets and languages as Pound did, all for the sake of

---

[2] *Collected Early Poems of Ezra Pound*, ed. Michael John King (New York: New Directions, 1976) 220.

creating great poetry in his own language. His highest aim was to promote a new Renaissance, and in an essay so titled in 1915 he proclaimed that "The first step of a renaissance, or awakening, is the importation of models for painting, sculpture, or writing."[3] In that endeavor, he said, the first principle to follow is that "We must learn what we can from the past, we must learn what other nations have done successfully under similar circumstances, we must think how they did it."[4]   He proceeded to put this principle into action in his poetry by drawing heavily from a vast pantheon of writers: from Greek and Latin poets like Homer, Sappho, Ovid, Propertius, and Horace, from the anonymous Anglo-Saxon poet of "The Seafarer," from ancient Chinese poets like Li Po (or Rihaku) and later Japanese haiku poets, from medieval French troubadours like Bertran de Born and Arnaut Daniel and from modern French Symbolist poets like Rimbaud and Corbière and Henri de Régnier, from medieval Italian poets like Dante and Cavalcanti, as well as from medieval English poets like Chaucer, Elizabethan poets like Ben Jonson or Edmund Waller, Victorian poets like Landor and Browning, or modern Irish poets like Yeats. Of course, Pound could not literally become one of these dead poets, but there is no doubt that he consciously absorbed their influences in making new poems of his own. In *The Pisan Cantos* he calls himself disparagingly "a swollen magpie in a fitful sun," as if he were a reckless acquisitor of stolen bits and pieces, but he was nevertheless the poet who succeeded where his earlier persona Hugh Selwyn Mauberley had failed, "to resuscitate / The dead art of poetry / To maintain 'the sublime,' in the old sense." Pound even claimed that his oft-repeated poetic slogan, "Make It New," was not his own invention. He said that what became the motto of Modernism had been translated from the inscription on an ancient Chinese emperor's bathtub. He never started *ex nihilo*; he specialized in creating new works from old.

In time, what seemed a miraculous feat of drawing new works out of old ones became the basis of a new poetic style, a movement for his age deliberately inspired by the models of previous ages. Not that he was always successful in his

---

[3] Pound, *Literary Essays*, 214.

[4] Pound. *Literary Essays*, 219.

borrowings, since there were more imitations than creations among his early poems, but by the time he had arrived at his mature style in *Ripostes* in 1912, he had founded an entirely new modern poetic movement which he called Imagism, and he had clearly mastered the technique of using influence creatively. His gift for learning foreign languages certainly helped him, since it was his ability to read poems in such diverse languages as Classical Greek, Chinese, and French, that enabled him to remake English poetic style from non-English sources.

Of the many examples of successful poetic reincarnations in Pound's poetry, there are three excellent works inspired by originals in three quite different languages which can stand as proof of his virtuosity. He converted a French Symbolist poem by Henri de Régnier into one of his best-known poems, "The Return"; he converted a short lyric by Ibycus from the Greek Anthology into his Imagist poem, "The Spring"; and he converted a Chinese poem of the Tang Dynasty, written by Li Po (or Rihaku, following Fenollosa) into "The River-Merchant's Wife: A Letter." By looking at literal English translations of each of these foreign poems, it is possible to see more plainly just how original Pound was in making them into new poems in English. It is a way of understanding a little better the mystery of how he transformed influence into inspiration, making a new poetic style which came to be called Modernism out of a variety of older poetic styles.

To take them in chronological order is to begin with "The Return," published in 1912 in *Ripostes*. No less an admirer than Yeats singled this poem out for praise. He did so when he spoke about the new free verse in Chicago in 1914 at a *Poetry* banquet in his honour. Yeats had such prestige as a poet that when he cited it as the best poem in the new style, he conferred on it the status of a classic. But though the poem seemed highly original, and is still baffling to most readers, it did have a source. We know that from René Taupin, who demonstrated that "The Return" was based on a little-known work by one of the lesser French Symbolists:

> In "The Return," Pound had sought to surpass the excellent title-poem of de Régnier's collection, *Medailles d'Argile*. Pound's admiration for the poem made him wish to produce an equivalent in English, if possible one that would be better than

the original. The rhythmical strength of the poem echoes that of de Régnier, and is obtained in the same manner: by frequent pauses and broken lines.[5]

To make it clear what Taupin was talking about, let me place a fairly literal translation (my own) of the de Régnier poem beside Pound's original poem:

Medals of Clay

I dreamed that the gods had spoken to me:
one streaming with seaweed and brine,
another heavy with grapes and wheat,
one winged,
handsome and shy,
a bare nude figure,
another veiled,
and still another
sang and plucked hemlock
and thoughts
and wreathed about his golden thyrsus
two serpents on a caduceus,
and another yet...

Then I said: here are flutes and baskets,
sink your teeth in the fruit;
hear the bees droning,
the humble sound
of willows being braided and roses being cut,
and again I said: listen,
listen,
behind the echo
someone stands, a universal life
with double bow and double torch
that is
divinely us ...

Unseen face! It's you I engrave
on silver medals, sweet as pale dawn,

---

[5] Taupin, 128.

on golden medals, burning like sun,
on brass medals, sombre as night;
something in all metal
shines clear as joy,
sounds deep as glory,
as love, as death;
the most beautiful things of fine clay
I have made, dry and fragile.

One by one, you counted them, smiling
and said: how cunning,
and passed on, smiling.

Yet none of you could see my hands
trembling with tenderness
that all the great terrestrial dream
lived in me to live in them,
and I engraved in sacred metal,
my gods,
who are the living face
that we smell in roses,
in the water, in the wind,
in the woods, in the sea,
in all things,
in our flesh—
and that are
divinely us.

Here is how Pound reworked de Régnier's French poem into a
new English poem:

The Return

See, they return; ah, see the tentative
        Movements, and the slow feet,
        The trouble in the pace and the uncertain
        Wavering!

See, they return, one, and by one,
With fear, as half-awakened;

As if the snow should hesitate
And murmur in the wind,
            and half turn back;
These were the "Wing'd-with-Awe,"
            Inviolable.

Gods of the wingèd shoe!
With them the silver hounds,
            sniffing the trace of air!

Haie! Haie!
        These were the swift to harry;
These the keen-scented;
These were the souls of blood.

Slow on the leash,
            pallid the leash men!

Taupin, in his study of Pound, compares the French Symbolist poem with the American Imagist poem to show that the French poet used several rhythmic patterns while "Pound fashioned a single movement, thus increasing the unity of his poem." I think Taupin meant that the rhythm of the French poem moves back and forth from long lines to short lines with deliberate breaks in the rhythmic continuity, while Pound's poem makes use of a strongly accented falling rhythm throughout, with a prevailing trochaic foot at the beginning of each line: "See, they return ... " etc. Yeats said that Pound had created a "real organic rhythm" in his poem which made free verse lyrical, and Yeats liked to read it aloud for that reason. To de Régnier's rhythm, Pound added the motion of the gods in their hesitant return to the earth, for Pound's poem describes them in action, whereas de Régnier pictures them simply appearing to men in visible form. It could be said that Pound's poem follows the feet of the gods, aurally, while de Régnier looks at their faces, visually. It could also be said that Pound describes the figures in motion, while de Régnier is engraving them on his tablets statically. It could even be said that Pound's poem reincarnates the gods, while de Régnier's poem memorializes them. Pound went beyond the French original to portray the physical presence of visionary beings. The French poet evokes a dreamlike image of a number of different Greek gods that are unnamed; Pound fashions a visible image that is of one main Greek god, Hermes, or Mercury, the messenger god with winged feet. He colors his image with words like "snow," "silver" and "pallid" that give tonal unity to the apparition. What Pound accomplishes in his poem forms an image more concentrated to the eye and more consistent to the ear than the original, and in so doing he succeeds in not merely translating but transforming the poem from French into English. As Taupin concluded from his study, the new poem in English is better than the earlier poem in French.

To look at a second example of Pound's use of influence as inspiration, he published "The Spring" in 1915 in a group of Imagist poems that appeared in *Poetry* magazine, basing it on an original lyric by Ibycus in the Greek Anthology. Here is a fairly literal English version of the poem, this time as translated by the classical scholar Richmond Lattimore:

The Spring

In spring time the Kydonian
quinces, watered by running streams,
there where the maiden nymphs have
their secret garden, and grapes that grow
round in shade of the tendriled vine,
ripen.
Now in this season for me
there is no rest from love.
Out of the hard bright sky,
a Thracian north wind blowing
with searing rages and hurt—dark,
pitiless, sent by Aphrodite—Love
rocks and tosses my heart.[6]

The Lattimore translation is accurate, but lacks strong emotion. Pound was able to fashion an entirely new English poem from the Greek original that seethes with emotion:

---

[6] *Greek Lyrics*, translated by Richmond Lattimore (Chicago: University of Chicago Press, 1960) 37-38.

The Spring

Ἦρι μεν ἀι τε κυδώνιαι
—Ibycus

Cydonian Spring with her attendant train,
Maelids and water-girls,
Stepping beneath a boisterous wind from Thrace,
Throughout this sylvan place
Spreads the bright tips,
And every vine-stock is
Clad in new brilliancies.

                    And wild desire
Falls like black lightning.
O bewildered heart,
Though every branch have back what last year lost,
She, who moved here among the cyclamen,
Moves only now a clinging tenuous ghost.

This poem is certainly one of Pound's brief lyrical masterpieces, and it is closely modeled on the original. His line is somewhat longer than Ibycus' Greek verses, or than the line Lattimore used in translating it into English, but the poem remains a love poem set in the spring, the traditional season for love. Pound transformed it into an English poem by deliberately altering it, by what some of his critics have called "creative mistranslation," converting "Kydonian quinces" into "Cydonian spring," and introducing "Maelids" or orchard-nymphs, into a poem where there were no such mythical beings, (they would have been spelled "Meliads" if they had been there). Thus, Pound has boldly changed the fruit of quinces into feminine spirits, a daring alteration of the original. He also transforms the "Thracian north wind blowing" in the second half of the original Greek poem into "a boisterous wind from Thrace" in the first half of his poem. Even more audaciously, he condenses the feeling of "no rest from love" and the sight of "the hard bright sky" into a single visual and emotional image that quite transcends the original: "And wild desire / Falls like black lightning." There is no such image in the Greek, and though springtime does induce an overpowering sexual urge in the Greek original, it is sent by Aphrodite, goddess of love, not by a dark thunderstorm as in Pound's poem, which seems to make the source of such supercharged sexual energy a heavenly bolt of lightning, suggesting Zeus, the male king of the gods, rather than the seductive Aphrodite.

It is at the end of Pound's "The Spring" that he makes the greatest conscious change, departing entirely from the Greek original to remake the poem, converting a sense of physical torment in love, "Love rocks and tosses my heart," into something quite different:

> She, who moved here among the cyclamen,
> Moves only now a clinging tenuous ghost.

The spirit of spring has undergone a metamorphosis in Pound's imagination. It has become the ghost of a girl now dead, whom the poet loved and whom he associates with the flowering cyclamen, who seems unwilling to let him go, holding him still in her "clinging tenuous" embrace. There is no hint of such a ghostly apparition in the Greek original, and so Pound has added an elegiac tone to the springtime love-lyric. Rhythmically, he has not followed the mainly tetrameter rhythm of the original Greek, nor a prosaic movement of the literal English version, but has created a new free verse rhythm with occasional rhymes ("Thrace" with "place" and "lost" with "ghost") that gives it continuous motion, except for the sharp break between the first and second stanzas that turns on the dramatic line "And wild desire / Falls like black lightning."

Thus Pound constructed a new poem in English out of an original poem in another language, and he did so often, notably when he produced his Chinese translations in *Cathay* in 1915. It was this book Eliot had in mind when he said that Pound was "the inventor of Chinese poetry for our time." They are all genuinely original poems in English, not mere translations, but probably the most celebrated is "The River-Merchant's Wife: A Letter." This poem is such a familiar anthology-piece to readers of Pound that they may not be prepared for a more literal version of the original—more literal, though Chinese is a picture-language rather than a phonetic language, and it is impossible to be completely literal with any translation of Chinese ideograms into English syllables. Here at any rate is the Chinese poem in a strictly literal translation:

Letter from Chang-Kan. I.
(A river-merchant's wife writes)

I would play, plucking flowers by the gate;
My hair scarcely covered my forehead, then.
You would come, riding on your bamboo horse,
And loiter about the bench with green plums for toys.
So we both dwelt in Chang-kan town,
We were two children, suspecting nothing.
At fourteen I became your wife,
And so bashful that I could never bare my face,
But hung my head, and turned to the dark wall;
You would call me a thousand times,
But I could not look back even once.

At fifteen I was able to compose my eyebrows,
And beg you to love me till we were dust and ashes.
You always kept the faith of Wei-sheng,
Who waited under the bridge, unafraid of death,
I never knew I was to climb the Hill of Wang-fu
And watch for you these many days.

I was sixteen when you went on a long journey,
Traveling beyond the Keu-Tang Gorge,
Where the giant rocks heap up the swift river,
And the rapids are not passable in May.
Did you hear the monkeys wailing
Up on the skyey height of the crags?

Do you know your foot-marks by our gate are old,
And each and every one is filled up with green moss?
The mosses are too deep for me to sweep away;
And already in the autumn wind the leaves are falling.
The yellow butterflies of October [the Eighth Month]
Flutter in pairs over the grass of the west garden.

My heart aches at seeing them ...
I sit sorrowing alone, and alas!
The vermilion of my face is fading.

Some day when you return down the river,
If you will write me a letter beforehand,
I will come to meet you—the way is not long—

I will come as far as the Long Wind Beach instantly.[7]

And here is Pound's familiar and far more memorable English version:

The River-Merchant's Wife: A Letter

While my hair was still cut straight across my forehead
I played about the front gate, pulling flowers.
You came by on bamboo stilts, playing horse,
You walked about my seat, playing with blue plums.
And we went on living in the village of Chokan:
Two small people, without dislike or suspicion.

At fourteen I married My Lord you.
I never laughed, being bashful.
Lowering my head, I looked at the wall.
Called to, a thousand times, I never looked back.

At fifteen I stopped scowling,
I desired my dust to be mingled with yours
Forever and forever and forever.
Why should I climb the look out?

At sixteen you departed,
You went into far Ku-to-yen, by the river of swelling eddies,
And you have been gone five months.
The monkeys make sorrowful noise overhead.
You dragged your feet when you went out.
By the gate now, the moss is grown, the different mosses,
Too deep to clear them away!
The leaves fall early this autumn, in wind.
The paired butterflies are already yellow with August
    Over the grass in the West garden;
    They hurt me. I grow older.

---

[7] *The Works of Li Po, The Chinese Poet*, translated by Shigeyoshi Obata (New York: Paragon, 1965) 152-53. Note that Chang-kan is a suburb of Nanking, and the Long Wind Beach, or Chang-feng Sha, is several hundred miles up river.

If you are coming down through the narrows of the river Kiang,
Please let me know beforehand,
And I will come out to meet you
As far as Cho-fu-sa.

"Creative mistranslation" may also come to mind in Pound's remaking of this poem, but the result is surely one of the finest of his poems, an original work based on a Chinese model. In writing it, Pound reduced the 36-line Chinese poem of Li Po to 29 lines, leaving out all reference to Wei-sheng, a legendary lover who drowned waiting for his love to appear, and changing Keu Tang Gorge to "far Ku-to-yen" as well as leaving "Long Wind Beach" untranslated, merely a mysterious Chinese name, "Cho-fu-sa," which serves to make the poem more ambiguous, and the distance between the lovers more indefinite. Pound interprets the "eighth month" to be August, as it would be in the Western calendar, though it may be later, September or October, in the Chinese calendar, but regardless of the exact month, the butterflies look yellower and no doubt dustier, whether it is the end of summer or early autumn. The figure of the Chinese girl is Pound's most original contribution to the poem, for he makes her plea more gentle and her feelings more restrained than in the Chinese original, evoking greater sympathy for her, as she waits in silence for her husband to return, but is clearly so eager to see him that she offers to go a long way down river from her village to meet him. Pound condenses the portrait of the River-Merchant's wife skillfully, so that she seems to gain in vulnerability and in self-restraint at the same time, a modest, appealing young woman who lives only for her husband and who is obviously desolate when he is absent, yet who conveys her longing for him by indirect suggestion—"the monkeys make sorrowful noise overhead"—rather than by direct description of her own feelings. The relatively bland and vague imagery of the Chinese original is replaced by the precision of Pound's translation, for in the more literal version of the original poem:

The yellow butterflies of October [the Eighth Month]
Flutter in pairs over the grass of the west garden.
My heart aches at seeing them!

This fairly objective description of a natural scene, followed by
a sudden outburst of emotion, is transformed by Pound into an
expression of deep yearning and inner anguish:

> The paired butterflies are already yellow with August
> Over the grass in the West garden;
> They hurt me. I grow older.

While the Chinese original only shows the motive for the
"letter"—the husband's frequent trips away from home—and
describes an unexceptional domestic scene in ordinary
language, Pound's poem (not strictly speaking a translation at
all) expresses an exquisite sense of how much the young wife
misses her husband, evoking a sympathetic feeling of admiration and affection in the reader.

These are just three instances of Pound's inspired use of
influence, drawn from poems in three quite different languages,
but they are enough to show how he discovered in himself a
capacity for making new poems in English that were both more
moving and more exact in their expression than the originals. It
was the secret of his genius that he learned how to transmit the
essence of foreign poetry into a vivid English that perfectly
matched the mood of the source without literally translating the
words. He was not exaggerating when he claimed late in his
career that he had managed "to gather from the air a live
tradition," because he knew instinctively what was alive in the
work of dead poets and could find the precise language to
capture it. Reading three of his best transformations, as they
might be called, from the many poems Pound fashioned in
English out of widely diverse originals, is to marvel all the more
at how he did it. One of his most enduring legacies was to make
new poetry out of old poetry, and in the process he showed how
a new English poetic style could be derived from totally
different foreign poems, poems which had nothing in common
until he translated them liberally, not literally, transforming
French and Greek and Chinese poems into distinctively English
poems with his signature on them as if he had written them
himself.

LIBRARY, UNIVERSITY OF CHESTER

3

THE IMAGIST DECADE, 1910-1920

Virginia Woolf once made the bold pronouncement that "on or about December, 1910, human character changed."[1] She was clearly exaggerating, but something important did change about 1910: English literary style. Virginia Woolf herself was one of the agents of change, with her experiments in stream-of-consciousness narration, but the more active agents of change were the Imagist poets: T. E. Hulme, Ezra Pound, Richard Aldington, H. D., F. S. Flint, William Carlos Williams, D. H. Lawrence, Amy Lowell, and John Gould Fletcher. Even Wallace Stevens, Marianne Moore, and T. S. Eliot, who weren't part of the original Imagist group, participated in changing the way English was written. They, together with stream-of-consciousness novelists, notably James Joyce and Virginia Woolf, did bring about a revolution in English poetry and prose. What emerged was a new style, a style which is still, a century later, the dominant style. (Postmodernism turned out to be a reaction against Modernism rather than a new movement in its own right.) What we can see more clearly now is that in the second decade of the twentieth century, a radical transformation occurred in the way English was used by its most gifted writers, and nothing comparable has happened since.

Modernism is the name for this revolution in English style, which was initiated in the decade between 1910 and 1920. The main influence was the Imagist movement, and so it could well be called The Imagist Decade. Virginia Woolf's arbitrary date of December, 1910, was about when the change started, but it took more than a decade to produce its full effect. Experiment led to achievement, and the modern style in fiction and poetry quickly distinguished itself from the conventional style of poetry and fiction written in English at the beginning of the century. The change began about 1910, though the year 1908 would be more exact, since the first identifiable Imagist poem, Hulme's "Autumn," appeared in a pamphlet called *For Christmas MDCCCCVIII*. Hulme did not yet know he was an Imagist, of

---

[1] Virginia Woolf, "Mr. Bennett and Mrs. Brown," in *The Captain's Death Bed and Other Essays* (New York: Harcourt Brace, 1950) 96.

course; he would have to wait for Pound to make that public in 1912. That was when Pound published *Ripostes*, with an Appendix he called "The Complete Poems of T. E. Hulme." It was meant to be taken as a joke, because for Hulme's entire corpus Pound offered only "Autumn" and four equally short poems, but he was serious about "the forgotten School of Images" that he credited Hulme with leading. Hulme had sensed what T. S. Eliot later stated, that "the situation of poetry in 1909 or 1910 was stagnant to a degree difficult for any young poet of to-day to imagine,"[2] and he set about to change it. Pound joined Hulme's group of young English poets in 1909, and by 1912 he had given a name to their experiments with poetic form. Eliot later acknowledged that modern poetry in English began with the Imagists and added "I was not there."[3] Eliot knew how much Pound had managed to accomplish in the five years before he arrived in London in 1914. To explain why the remarkable change in English poetry could have occurred in those few short years, Eliot would say, "I look back to the dead year 1908, and I observe with satisfaction that the current of French poetry which sprang from Baudelaire is one which has . . . affected all English poetry that matters."[4]

Eliot was connecting Imagism with Symbolism, recognizing that there had been an earlier poetic movement in another language that had started the change of style, and that the main force of French Symbolist influence on English had been borne by the Imagists, as Pound had christened them. Eliot had taken his cue from Pound, and had himself become a major contributor to the change in English poetic style that incorporated both Symbolism and Imagism. His view of the convergence of these two movements agreed, as we have seen, with René Taupin's conclusion, after careful study, that the 'image' of the Imagists and the 'symbol' of the Symbolists differed little, except in brevity.[5]

---

[2] T. S. Eliot, "Introduction," xiii.

[3] T. S. Eliot, "American Literature and the American Language," 58.

[4] T. S. Eliot, Review of *Baudelaire and the Symbolists* by Peter Quennell, *Criterion*, IX (January 1930): 359.

[5] Taupin, 93.

Around 1910, then, Imagism as a movement resulted from an unlikely international collaboration between the Poets' Club in London and the French Symbolists in Paris—"But," as F. S. Flint, who was well acquainted with both groups, acknowledged later, "it was not until 1912 that the word Imagiste (the descent of which is obvious) was invented by Mr. Ezra Pound."[6] In fact, it was in 1912 that the name was used twice by Pound, both times in its French spelling Imagiste: first in *Ripostes* (his poems with a French title), and secondly, in the pen-name he gave Hilda Doolittle, when he signed her three short poems "H. D. Imagiste" and sent them off to Harriet Monroe in Chicago to be published in the new *Poetry* magazine. What was notable about his use of the term twice in the same year, applied first to his own poetry and that of T. E. Hulme, then to the poetry of H. D. and Richard Aldington, was that Pound was thinking of the Imagists as a coherent group of poets who had been meeting and sharing poems ever since 1909, that they were English as well as American, and that a revolution was already under way in the theory and practice of English poetry. So when he appended to his own poems in *Ripostes* the five short poems which he called "The Complete Poetical Works of T. E. Hulme," and noted that "As for the future, Les Imagistes, the descendants of the forgotten school of 1909 [the "School of Images,"] have that in their keeping," he was making literary history.

Pound, probably alone among writers of English, believed as early as 1912 that the future of literature was predictable, and that, as he later put it, "we had as much right to a group name, at least as much right, as a number of French 'schools' proclaimed by Mr. Flint in the August number of Harold Monro's magazine [*Poetry and Drama*] for 1912."[7] Thus he could place the future confidently in the hands of the Imagists, though in 1912 Imagism as a movement was largely in his head, no more than a convenient name for a few writers who had been meeting in London off and on since 1909. So to call 1910-1920 "The Imagist Decade" is only to recognize, in the first decade of the twenty-first century, what a significant difference in English style the Imagists made at the

---

[6] F. S. Flint, unpublished draft of an article on "Imagism" written about 1918, in the Humanities Research Center at the University of Texas in Austin.

[7] Ezra Pound, "A Retrospect," 3.

beginning of the last century. It is obvious that no comparable change has happened since.

Pound did not claim ownership of the new movement. He gave precedence to other poets as the first Imagists, citing the work of T. E. Hulme and H. D. rather than his own. Hulme had been the leader of the Poets' Club that Pound called the School of Images, had published the first unofficial Imagist poem in 1908, and had engaged in poetic experiments that centered on the Image, but it was Pound who in 1912 named the new poetic movement Les Imagistes. And it was Pound who made "H. D. Imagiste" the first poet of the new movement in the pages of *Poetry* magazine in 1913. She was as surprised as anyone by that sudden transformation, as she testified much later in *End to Torment: A Memoir of Ezra Pound*. She had shown Pound three short poems in the British Museum Tea Room in the fall of 1912. The poems were "Hermes of the Ways," "Priapus (The Orchard)," and "Oread," all imitations of Classical Greek lyrics. Pound quickly edited them, scrawled "H. D. Imagiste" at the bottom, and sent them off to Harriet Monroe at *Poetry* magazine in Chicago, where they appeared in January, 1913, as "Verses, Translations, and Reflections of 'The Anthology'" rather than as Imagist poems. Richard Aldington, who later married H. D., agreed with her that Pound was the only begetter of Imagism. Like her, he was one of the original Imagists, but they had become "Amygists," as Pound nicknamed them, when Amy Lowell took over the group and edited three anthologies she called *Some Imagist Poets*, in 1915, 1916, and 1917. Those anthologies caused some readers to think she was the inventor of Imagism, but as Aldington wrote in a letter to Pound in 1928, she had not been there in the beginning. He clarified a still controversial point of literary history by saying:

> My version is that Hulme was a sort of distant ancestor, that you invented Imagism as a word, that the "movement" was decided upon by the three of us, at your suggestion, in a Kensington tea-shop, to launch H.D. We all published "Imagist" poems with Harriet before Amy was

> heard of. The first Imagist anthology was your
> idea and edited by you.[8]

There is only one slight discrepancy between Aldington's account
and H. D.'s about the origin of Imagism, and that is where the
historic meeting took place. No doubt the three poets had
discussed the possibility of an Imagist movement in the spring of
1912, "in a Kensington tea-shop," as Aldington remembered it,
and H. D. remembered that in the fall of that year, in the tea shop
of the British Museum, Pound seized the opportunity to launch
the new movement with a few of her poems.

The question of who deserved the most credit for
inventing Imagism was in some doubt, partly because Pound
himself had deferred to Hulme and then to H. D., when he first
used the name Imagiste in 1912. It was also known that, after he
had edited the first anthology, *Des Imagistes*, in 1914, Pound
abandoned Imagism for a new movement he called Vorticism,
leaving Amy Lowell in charge of the later anthologies. But there
has never really been any doubt that, without Pound, there would
have been no Imagist movement, for as T. S. Eliot put it in his
tribute to Pound in 1945:

> Pound did not create the poets: but he created a
> situation in which, for the first time, there was a
> "modern movement in poetry" in which English
> and American poets collaborated, knew each
> other's works, and influenced each other.[9]

The "modern movement in poetry" began with Imagism,
as Eliot acknowledged, even though he did not meet Pound in
London until the fall of 1914 after Pound had left the Imagists.
But while Eliot continued to regard Imagism as only a passing
phase in Pound's career, it was in truth integral to his whole
development as a poet, as has been ably attested by later critics,

---

[8] Richard Aldington, letter to Ezra Pound (dated 7/8/28), in *Ezra Pound*

Perspectives: Essays in Honor of his Eightieth Birthday, edited by Noel Stock

(Chicago: Henry Regnery, 1965; reprinted by Greenwood Press, Westport,

Conn., 1977) 123.

[9] T. S. Eliot, "Ezra Pound (1946)" 29.

among them Herbert Read, a sometime Imagist himself, who said in a tribute to Pound in 1965:

> We might explain Pound's later development by saying that he began with free verse of a vaguely rhetorical kind, and arrived at a specific kind of free verse to which he gave the name "Imagism." Imagism differs from Whitmanesque and other varieties of free verse in insisting on a concreteness of imagery, and on a tight musical or rhythmical structure. Nothing is in a certain sense less free than good free verse, for it achieves an exact correspondence between the verbal and rhythmical structure of the verse and the mood or emotion to be expressed. The result is a quality which Mr. Eliot has recently called "transparent"—"that is to say, you listen not to poetry as poetry but to the meaning of poetry." In Pound's words, you get rid of the ornament. And when you are rid of the ornament you are left with the image, the direct percept.[10]

Read's view that Pound was an Imagist throughout his career, not merely for a few influential years, has been corroborated by other critics, notably by the American poet and critic Robert Penn Warren. Warren belonged to a later poetic school—one which called itself the Fugitives—not to the Imagists. This school was based in Nashville, Tennessee, a provincial Southern city, not in a world capital like London, and it came afterward and in many ways opposed the Anglo-American Imagists, but Warren much later in his career gave tribute to Pound, saying in a radio broadcast in 1955:

> He was an Imagist, and in one sense remains an Imagist...his sense of images, the freshness, of the physical world, of the things seen, the things smelt, the things heard. There's no poet that more powerfully captures and re-presents to us that aspect of the world...In Canto after Canto, these flashes, pure and morning-bright, of the physical

---

[10] Herbert Read, "Ezra Pound" in *Ezra Pound Perspectives*, 14.

world, are probably the thing that will make
Pound's work as abiding as any we have in our
time.[11]

Historically speaking, Imagism was the beginning of literary
Modernism in English, which was led by Pound, but which drew
together a number of writers, British and American, novelists as
well as poets (Pound included Ford Madox Ford and James Joyce
in *Des Imagistes*), and derived its name as well as some of its
poetic theory principally from the French Symbolists, or
Symbolistes, not from any earlier English or American poetic
tradition.
  Les Imagistes learned from Les Symbolistes what they
could not have learned from poets writing in English at the
beginning of the century. Not all English and American poets
were "stagnant" at that time: there had been experimentalists like
Whitman and Stephen Crane among the Americans; innovators
like Kipling, Housman, and Yeats, among the British. Pound
knew their work, as he knew the long tradition of world poetry.
He had made a famous "Pact" with Whitman, had publicly praised
Yeats as the only poet in English worth serious study when he
arrived in London in 1908, and had written witty parodies of
Kipling and Housman and even Yeats. Yet the inspiration for
Imagism came from France. Pound's spelling of the name *Des
Imagistes* was a deliberate allusion: it was Amy Lowell who
translated it into *Some Imagist Poets* after Pound had left the
movement. So the French Symbolist poets were clearly foremost
in the minds of Pound and other young English and American
poets who started Imagism.
  Why was this so? First of all, the French Symbolists were
a movement, and there was no such movement in English poetry.
Even Laura Riding and Robert Graves, in their *Survey of
Modernist Poetry* in 1928, while taking a generally unfavorable
view of both Imagism and Modernism, admitted that "The
Imagists had decided beforehand the kind of poetry that was

---

[11] Robert Penn Warren, in "A Tribute to Ezra Pound," radio broadcast for his

70th birthday, Dec., 1955. A transcript of this broadcast from the Yale

University station is in the Humanities Research Center of the University of

Texas at Austin.

wanted for the time: a poetry to match certain up-to-date movements in music and art."[12] In fact, English writers had little to do with movements before the Imagists (the Pre-Raphaelites were admired as painters first and poets second), but the French affinity for artistic movements was well established, and Hulme, Flint, and Pound liked the appeal of the avant-garde in France, where the Impressionists dominated painting, the Realists and Naturalists dominated fiction, and the Symbolists dominated poetry. They saw no English or American equivalent, and having read Arthur Symons's book in 1902 on *The Symbolist Movement in France*—with an Introduction by Yeats, himself an Irish Symbolist—they wanted to promote something like it in England and America. Hulme and Flint knew the early twentieth-century philosophical and poetic trends in France better than Pound did, when he first met them at the Eiffel Tower Restaurant in Soho in April, 1909, but it was Pound's ingenuity that gave the new movement its own name and its first official poems in 1912, as well as its own principles in 1913.

Pound was an originator; he was not a mere imitator. He realized that an English, American, or even an Anglo-American, Symbolism would not provide enough impetus for new poetry, and so he invented a new name, Imagism, taking his cue from Hulme, who had taken it from Henri Bergson's theory of the Image, and then deduced the three "rules" of Imagism from French sources: 1) "Direct treatment of the 'thing,' whether subjective or objective," that is, the Image as subject, stemming from the Symbol of the Symbolists and from the central theory of memory-images in Bergson's philosophy, 2) "To use absolutely no word that does not contribute to the presentation," that is, verbal precision, stemming from Flaubert's *le mot juste* ("the exact word"), and 3)"As regarding rhythm, to compose in the sequence of the musical phrase, not in sequence of a metronome," that is, free verse, a literal translation of the French Symbolist technique of *vers libre*.

Pound came up with the three cardinal rules of Imagism in March 1913 in *Poetry* magazine, shortly after the three poems of "H. D. Imagiste" appeared, and offered a one-sentence definition of the key term: "An Image is that which presents an intellectual

---

[12] Laura Riding and Robert Graves, *A Survey of Modernist Poetry* (originally published 1928, reprinted New York: Haskell House, 1969) 117.

and emotional complex in an instant of time." The definition, like the rules, he derived from French poetry and philosophy—from the Symbolists, with their notion of the poem as a fusion of subjective and objective realities, and from Bergson (via Hulme), with his notion that memory-images link to make up the chief continuity of mental life.

Pound may also have been influenced in his definition of Imagism by American psychologists like William James, who had spoken of interior mental life as a "stream of consciousness," for when Pound tied the Image to the notion of a "complex," he said he was using it as an American psychologist—not William James but the less well known Bernard Hart—might understand it, since both James and Hart, like Freud, took account of the unconscious or subconscious impulses at work in human thought. What is significant is that Imagism, which came from a variety of models, not only French but Greek and Japanese, came also from a composite of ideas, scientific and philosophical as well as artistic, most of which were French and none of which was original with either Hulme or Pound. What was original was putting them together and forming an intellectual movement of English and American poets. What is more, it worked, and worked so well that what Stephen Spender would later call "the seminal image" became the essential building-block of the new poetry.[13] And Spender, an English poet of a younger generation, contended that, "The aims of the Imagist movement in poetry provide the archetype of a modern creative procedure." Not only were new and different poems written because the Imagists existed, but, as Spender also pointed out, the new fiction of Joyce and Virginia Woolf used a succession of brief images to describe the inner working of the human mind, making stream-of-consciousness narrative techniques an extension into the novel of the poetic techniques of Imagism.

Thus, we may say that if Imagism started to emerge in 1908 when Hulme published "Autumn" in a Poets' Club pamphlet and then in 1909 led a revolt from the Poets' Club toward "a lot of talk about the Image," it did not really become a movement until 1912, when Pound gave it a name, "Les Imagistes"—meaning H. D., Aldington, and himself—the descendants of "the School of Images" that Hulme had earlier led, and Imagism did not become a definite school until 1913, when the first poems by "H. D.

---

[13] See Spender, 110-15.

Imagiste" appeared in the January issue of *Poetry*, followed in March by the three rules of Imagism, originally dictated by Pound but quoted by Flint in his essay on "Imagisme,"[14] and the definition of the Image by Pound in "A Few Don'ts by an Imagiste." To see how, after such a haphazard start, Imagism dominated the poetry and even the prose of the whole decade surrounding the First World War, we need to look at the successive Imagist anthologies, *Des Imagistes*, edited by Pound in 1914, his *Catholic Anthology* in 1915, and *Some Imagist Poets*, edited by Amy Lowell in 1915, 1916, and 1917, as well as at the pages of such periodicals as *Poetry* and *The Little Review* in Chicago, *Others* in New York, and *The Egoist* and *Blast* in London.

These were the avant-garde publications of the Imagist decade in English, and any reader looking through them now can clearly see the prominence of early Imagists like H. D., Pound, Aldington, and Flint and later Imagists like Lowell, Fletcher, and Lawrence. A reader can also see the emergence of major new poets like William Carlos Williams, Marianne Moore, Wallace Stevens, and T. S. Eliot, all Americans with distinctive individual styles who did not become Imagist poets but experimented successfully with the Imagist form—the short, free-verse lyric centered on poetic imagery. Such poems as Williams's "Metric Figure," Moore's "To a Steam Roller," Stevens's "Domination of Black," and Eliot's "Preludes" are certainly of the Imagist type, and they came out in the magazines where Imagism was introduced to the sophisticated reading public of the day. And in the pages of *The Egoist* in 1914-15 and *The Little Review* in 1918-21, are to be found later poems by Yeats like "The Magi" and "The Coat," which were short enough and pictorial enough to be in key with the practice of the Imagists. There, too, are the chapters of Joyce's *A Portrait of the Artist as a Young Man*, serialized in *The Egoist*, and *Ulysses*, serialized in *The Little Review* until the magazine was stopped by the censors. This new fiction appealed at once to readers accustomed to Imagist poetry, who were receptive to Joyce's new stream-of-consciousness narration. Reading these pages now reveals the simultaneous emergence of Imagism and Modernism, and if at the end of the

---

[14] See "Documents on Imagism from the Papers of F. S. Flint" by Christopher

Middleton in *The Review*, no. 15 (April 1965). 35-51.

decade Imagism grew fainter while Modernism grew stronger, the Imagist technique was not abandoned but simply extended into longer and longer works. Verbal brevity gradually gave way to extended verbal intensity, and the single image grew into a mosaic of images, so that as the 1910s progressed to the 1920s, the results were Pound's *Cantos*, Eliot's *The Waste Land*, and Joyce's *Ulysses*.

We are a little beyond the Imagist Decade, but it was Ezra Pound's judgment in 1922, when he had reduced the manuscript to its published form, that "Eliot's *Waste Land* is I think the justification of the 'movement,' of our modern experiment, since 1900."[15] The success of Imagism had led to what might be called Eliot's Super-Imagist modern epic. But already, there had been Pound's ironic self-portrait, *Hugh Selwyn Mauberley*, which was published in 1920, and which was a poetic summing up of the Imagist Decade, both its successes and its failures. Pound had summed up the decade in prose in his essay, "A Retrospect," which appeared earlier, in 1918, in *Pavannes and Divisions*.

If Pound deserves credit for starting the movement in 1912 and writing its epitaph in 1920, he was only one of many Imagist poets, who learned from his precepts and examples and helped make the Imagist Decade the most revolutionary creative period of the century, so far as literature in English is concerned. These poems vindicate Pound's claim, in "A Retrospect," in 1918, that "Perhaps a few good poems have come from the new method, and if so it is justified."[16]

There were more than a few good poems produced by the new method. Among them are Hulme's poems, more than the five Pound called "The Complete Poetical Works of T. E. Hulme," but justifying Pound's comment, when he appended them to Ripostes, that "In publishing his *Complete Poetical Works* at thirty, Mr. Hulme has sent an enviable example to many of his contemporaries who have had less to say."[17]

---

[15] Pound, *Letters*, 180.

[16] Pound, "A Retrospect," 3.

[17] Ezra Pound, "The Complete Poetical Works of T. E. Hulme," appendix to *Personae: The Collected Poems of Ezra Pound* (New York: Boni & Liveright, 1926) 251.

Hulme's poetic works, along with his essays on poetry, brief though they are, give him a unique position as one of the progenitors of Modern Poetry: he was a philosophical Imagist at his best. The most natural Imagist was H. D., whose style and form seemed to suit the movement from the beginning, praised especially by Pound for being always "hard" and "clear." She owed more to the Greek Anthology than any of the Imagists, but her subjects bore her own stamp of originality, as in one of her earliest poems, called "Epigram (After the Greek)":

> The golden one is gone from the banquets;
> She, beloved of Atimetus,
> The swallow, the bright Homonoea;
> Gone the dear chatterer.

The Greek names "Atimetus" and "Homonoea" are obscure (I once asked a professor of Greek to translate them into English, and he told me they were "untranslatable"), but they imply a Classical Greek setting for this brief elegy. It describes a young girl now dead, but fondly remembered as a "golden one," a "swallow," and a "dear chatterer." What H. D. captured in this short lyric is the image of a girl who was once loved for her brightness and delicacy, now only a memory. Pound's nickname for H. D. was "Dryad," a wood nymph; it is the sort of spirit that inhabits all her poetry.

The Imagist poems of Richard Aldington sometimes echoed the Greek Anthology as did those of H. D., but with an edge of wit, as in:

Evening

> The chimneys, rank on rank,
> Cut the clear sky;
> The moon
> With a rag of gauze about her loins
> Poses among them, an awkward Venus—
>
> And here am I looking wantonly at her
> Over the kitchen sink.

The setting of this poem is a large city with rows of chimneys, and the mood is urbane. It pictures a domesticated husband washing the dishes and looking over the sink at the moon, which he visualizes as the goddess of love, revealing himself as incurably and absurdly romantic. Venus, both the moon and the love goddess, gives it a Classical reference, but it is an unlikely modern love poem with a sophisticated twist, seven lines of ironic Imagism.

T. S. Eliot arrived in London too late to be an Imagist, but he had written his "Preludes" in Boston before he met Pound, and originally called them "Preludes in Roxbury," named for a Boston suburb near Cambridge. They were four short poems in the Imagist mode, as Pound recognized when he published them in *Blast* in July 1915. Soon after he met Pound and settled in London, he wrote what might be called a fifth "Prelude," and published it in the September 1915 issue of *Poetry*:

Morning at the Window

They are rattling breakfast plates in basement kitchens,
And along the trampled edges of the street
I am aware of the damp souls of housemaids
Sprouting despondently at area gates.
The brown waves of fog toss up to me
Twisted faces from the bottom of the street,
And tear from a passer-by with muddy skirts
An aimless smile that hovers in the air
And vanishes along the level of the roofs.

Blast was the organ of the Vorticist movement which followed the Imagist movement, but what we know about this poem makes it definitely Imagist. Eliot set the poem in the Russell Square neighborhood of London, near the British Museum, where he briefly resided in the fall of 1914 when he first met Pound, before going on to Oxford to continue his philosophical studies. In a letter of 8 Sept. 1914, to his brother Henry Ware Eliot, Jr., Eliot described the view from the window of his rented room at 28 Bedford Place, where he was living at the time he met Pound. Looking out in unseasonably hot weather, he saw "a dreadful old woman, her skirt trailing on the street," who was singing as "the housemaid resumes her conversation at the area gates."[18] He finished "Morning at the Window" later at Oxford, and included "the damp souls of housemaids / Sprouting despondently at area gates," and "a passer-by with muddy skirts," who is not singing, but is displaying "an aimless smile that hovers in the air /And vanishes along the level of the roofs." In the course of writing it, Eliot revised the wording of this poem slightly, because it was too much like the wording of one of Pound's short poems. Pound confided in a letter to Marianne Moore that Eliot had first described the housemaids' souls as "*Hanging* despondently at area gates," but changed it to the more unusual "Sprouting" because Pound, in a poem called "Les Millwins," had spoken of the souls of women at a ballet as "lying along the upper seats."[19] Thus Pound's influence on Eliot preceded his editing of *The Waste Land*, yet the poem is certainly Eliot's own; it is the image of a nameless city-dweller looking out his window at the prospect of another dreary day among "damp souls" and "twisted faces," ending with the foggy image of a woman "with muddy skirts" whose smile is aimless and distant, no relief from the sordid urban scene. In Eliot's handling of it, Imagism became metaphysical: it penetrated into the monotony of city life even before he wrote *The Waste Land*, mirroring the emptiness of an urban existence where the soul seemed to wither inside the body.

William Carlos Williams had been Pound's friend at Penn, before he arrived in London, but he and Pound kept in touch, and it was Williams who provided a poetic tribute to the Imagists as an influence on his own poetry, using for his title the French spelling which Pound preferred:

Aux Imagistes

I think I have never been so exalted
As I am now by you,
O frost bitten blossoms,

---

[18] *The Selected Letters of T. S. Eliot*, Vol. I, 1898-1922, edited by Valerie Eliot (New York: Harcourt Brace Jovanovich, 1988) 55.

[19] Robert Coltrane, "The Imagist Relationship between Pound's 'Les Millwins' and Eliot's 'Morning at the Window,'" *Paideuma*, Vol. 18, No. 3 (Winter 1989): 123-28.

That are unfolding your wings
From out the envious black branches.

Bloom quickly and make much of the sunshine
The twigs conspire against you!
Hear them!
They hold you from behind!

You shall not take wing
Except wing by wing, brokenly,
And yet—
Even they
Shall not endure for ever.

Though Williams had stayed at home in New Jersey to pursue his medical career, while his poet friends Pound and H. D. had moved to London, he became much more than a provincial American poet. Pound chose one of Williams's poems for *Des Imagistes* and published "Aux Imagistes" in the *Egoist* magazine in London in December, 1914. Williams was determinedly American, but he liked being one of the Imagists from a distance, drawing his images from nature, not from the city, and in his tribute making a tree the metaphor for the poetic tradition and the Imagists "frost bitten blossoms." The extended metaphor moves from nature to culture, and implies that the new poetic movement of Imagism, though it might appear to be "nipped in the bud," is a vital creative force at work in the English language which is sure to bear fruit in the future.

Despite abandoning Imagism for Vorticism, Pound expressed his satisfaction with what the Imagist movement had accomplished when he wrote "A Retrospect" in 1918, though his judgment of its success was harsher when he wrote *Hugh Selwyn Mauberley* in 1920:

The age demanded an image
Of its accelerated grimace,
Something for the modern stage,
Not at any rate an Attic grace;

Pound, in creating the fictional American poet Mauberley who had come to London, like Pound, and tried "to resuscitate the dead art / Of poetry," by taking French poetry and prose as his model,

("His true Penelope was Flaubert,") depicted him as a failure. But we cannot take Pound's words literally, because there are ironies in his poem which are not in his prose, and so we must weigh his poetic farewell to London in 1920 against his summing up of Imagist accomplishments in "A Retrospect" in 1918. If we do, then we may see that the Imagist Decade did not end in defeat, as *Mauberley* seems to say, but issued rather in the triumph of Modernism, which through mainly Imagist techniques of verbal concentration and rhythmic freedom produced new and original forms in which to express devastatingly critical views of modern civilization.

    In "A Retrospect," his prose summary, Pound restated all the Imagist principles he had published in *Poetry* magazine in 1913, and expressed regret that "This school has since been 'joined' or 'followed' by numerous people who, whatever their merits, do not show any signs of agreement with the second specification," (i.e., "Use absolutely no word which does not contribute to the presentation"). Pound clearly meant that the "Amygists," as he had nicknamed them, were prolix in comparison with the earlier *Imagistes*, losing some of the intensity of the Imagist poem, but his criticism was intended as a corrective which might set Imagism back on track, because Pound was convinced that the principles and practice had been right. He was still urging poets to "Go in fear of abstractions" as he had in his Imagist period, to remember that "the proper and perfect symbol is the natural object," to master free verse so that poetry would be more musical, to work toward the ideal of "absolute rhythm," or "a rhythm in poetry which corresponds exactly to the emotion or shade of emotion to be expressed." In short, Pound in 1918, though he had left the Imagists behind, was insisting nevertheless on the permanent value of Imagist principles, on the importance of learning the art of poetry and uniting "that art again to its sustenance, life," by avoiding "convention and cliché" and choosing fresh images. And he held up for emulation the poems of Richard Aldington and H. D. in *Des Imagistes*, those of other Imagists like Williams and Joyce, as well as those of the later Yeats and the early Eliot.

    If Pound in theory at least was still an Imagist, in practice he was writing longer poems, notably *The Cantos*, but most often by the accumulation of lyrical images rather than by the adoption of narrative or dramatic forms, just as Eliot was doing at the same time. Both of these radical experimenters suddenly took up rhymed and metered stanzas as an antidote to free verse, and placed inside them a persona or alter ego rather than an impersonal voice, yet their poems were still focused on verbal images, Eliot in his Sweeney poems and Pound in Mauberley. For while Pound was presenting his figure of Mauberley as a failed poet, adding one more tombstone to the graveyard of failed artists like the earlier Pre-Raphaelites and "The Tragic Generation" Yeats wrote about in his *Autobiography*, he was also presenting Mauberley as a poet who upheld, however ineffectually, Pound's own Imagist principles:

> —Given that is his "fundamental passion,"
> This urge to convey the relation
> Of eye-lid and cheek-bone
> By verbal manifestation;

Thus if Pound found himself at odds with what "the age demanded," which was "an image of its accelerated grimace" instead of the kind of sharp critical observation of life which the Imagist poem made possible, and if Hugh Selwyn Mauberley thought his efforts futile:

> "I was
> And I no more exist;
> Here drifted
> An hedonist,"

Ezra Pound the author of *Mauberley* was not a failure like his persona. He could sacrifice his fictional poet to "the tawdry cheapness," of "a botched civilization," refusing to follow the advice of his fictional critic, Mr. Nixon, to "give up verse, my boy, / There's nothing in it," and instead going on with his poetic experiments, maintaining that a new Renaissance had taken place in the decade preceding *Mauberley*, the Imagist Decade in which he had led the way. Eliot later affirmed what was no longer in doubt, that Pound had more to do with the twentieth century revolution in poetry than any other individual,[20] and if we take "A Retrospect" and *Hugh Selwyn Mauberley* as the joint summing up, in prose and poetry, in 1918 and 1920, of what the Imagist movement accomplished during the second decade of the

---

[20] Eliot, "Introduction," xi.

twentieth century, we may safely conclude that the movement ended by transcending itself, being assimilated as a set of techniques—concreteness of imagery, concentration of meaning, and rhythmic variety—into the longer poems of Pound and Eliot and the stream-of-consciousness novels of Joyce and Woolf. The Imagist Decade ended in fact with the triumph of Modernism in literature, a triumph for which it had prepared the way.

4

POUND AS A MODERN TROUBADOUR

When F. S. Flint published his "History of Imagism" in 1915, he looked on Ezra Pound as a rash American intruder on the English literary scene, for though Pound had been invited to join the original School of Images in April 1909 on the strength of a new book of poems, Flint said that Pound was "full of his troubadours but I do not remember that he did more than an attempt to illustrate (or refute) our theories occasionally with their example."[1] Flint was not the only Englishman who saw Pound as a foreigner disturbing the peace, for when Pound boomed out "Sestina: Altaforte," speaking with the voice of the medieval French troubadour Bertran de Born, at the Tour Eiffel restaurant in London, the waiters quickly placed a screen around the table to shield the other diners from the noise he made.

It is worth remembering now, when many readers have come to look on Pound as the leader of a revolution in poetic style which changed the shape of English poetry, that he was not easily assimilated into the Poets Club dissidents, of whom T. E. Hulme was the acknowledged leader, those Pound later called "the School of Images, which may or may not have existed."[2] Nor could he easily claim, as he later did, that "as for the future, Les Imagistes, the descendants of the forgotten school of 1909, have that in their keeping," for Flint was around to remind him that when he arrived in London he knew little about Les Symbolistes, the original modern movement of French poets whose title Pound was consciously adapting, while Flint knew a great deal about them. Pound knew much more about the medieval troubadours, because they had been his poetic heroes when he came to London, and in 1910, before he had persuaded a somewhat reluctant group of English poets to join him in founding Imagism, he had published a book of poems called *Provença* and a book of criticism called *The Spirit of Romance*, both of which were centered on the troubadours. It

---

[1] Flint, "History of Imagism," *Egoist* 11 (May 1, 1915): 70.

[2] Ezra Pound, *Personae: The Shorter Poems*, Rev. Ed. Lea Baechler & A. Walton Litz (New York: New Directons, 1990) 266.

seems fair to say that at the start of his career, Pound wanted most of all to be identified as a modern troubadour, and he directed his considerable poetic talent, his formidable learning, and his boundless energy toward creating just such a persona.

If it is easy now to think of Pound as upsetting the staid English literary scene with his revolutionary poetics, it is less easy to explain his initial fascination with the medieval French troubadours. Yet there is no doubt that in his mind the troubadours came first, not the Imagists. For one thing, he genuinely liked their poetry, comparing it with the best of the Greek lyrics: "in Greece and in Provence the poetry attained its highest rhythmic and metrical brilliance," he wrote in 1913 in his essay on "The Tradition,"[3] at the very moment when he was busy launching Imagism as a new movement. He liked the aesthetic distance from the strictly English tradition which was provided by the Provençal language, a language which was obsolete and which few took the trouble to learn. He even joked, in a 1920 essay on Arnaut Daniel, about the obscurity of the French troubadours, jesting that "the twenty-three students of Provençal and the seven people seriously interested in the technic and aesthetic of verses may communicate with me in person."[4] He had been a scholar of Romance languages for over a decade, ever since his student days at Hamilton College and the University of Pennsylvania, and had been led to the troubadours by Dante, the Italian poet he most admired, who had regarded the Provençal poets as prior masters of poetic form, for as Pound wrote "it may be noted that the canzon of Provence became the canzone of Italy." Pound knew that Dante had praised the Italian troubadour poet Sordello and the French troubadour poet Arnaut Daniel in his *Purgatorio*, and had given a memorable dramatic portrait in his *Inferno* of Bertran de Born, who was vividly depicted as a "stirrer up of strife," forced to carry his severed head like a lantern in his hand. Most unforgettably of all to Pound, Dante had said in the 26th Canto of the *Purgatorio* that Arnaut Daniel *fu miglior fabbro nel parlar materno*, that is, he "was the better craftsman in the mother tongue." Though many poets followed Pound as an Imagist, few poets shared his interest in the French troubadours. Eliot was

---

[3] Pound, *Literary Essays*, 91.

[4] Pound, *Literary Essays*, 115.

the great exception, for, having come to a new appreciation of Dante through Pound, he understood Pound's reverence for the troubadours, and placed as an epigraph to The Waste Land: "For Ezra Pound, *il miglior fabbro*," implying that what Arnaut Daniel had been to Dante, Pound had been to Eliot.

Even beyond his liking for troubadour poetry and his knowledge of its importance to Dante, Pound was aware of the original meaning of the word *troubadour*, from the Provençal word *trobar* (modern French *trouver*) "to find," or "to discover." He wanted to be the sort of discoverer the Provençal troubadours had been much earlier, finding new poetic forms which in his case would lead him eventually to found the Imagist movement. "The Troubadours were melting the common tongue and fashioning it into new harmonies,"[5] he wrote with admiration in *The Spirit of Romance* in 1910, and he recognized the Provençal poets for their rhythmical invention and the intricacy of their rhymes. He also liked the phrase many others regarded as opaque, *trobar clus*, "closed or obscure verse," a phrase often applied to the poetry of Arnaut Daniel, since it signified the esoteric and mystical love poem written by certain Provençal troubadour poets of the twelfth and thirteenth centuries. Dante admired the mystical element in Arnaut Daniel's poetry as much as Pound did, and what Pound spoke of as "the involved forms, and the veiled meanings in the *trobar clus*" made it all the more desirable in his eyes, for it meant that a lyric tradition had arisen in Provence so skilled that even Dante acknowledged its priority.

Pound was always seeking origins, and for him the troubadours were genuine originators, just as he himself hoped to be: "Any study of European poetry is unsound if it does not commence with a study of that art in Provence,"[6] he wrote. So when Pound came to London from America by way of Venice, he hoped to start a new lyric tradition with the French troubadours as his models. Fortunately, he soon met T. E. Hulme and F. S. Flint, the English poets of the School of Images, who provided him with contemporary theories, and with practice in poetic forms, which he could fashion into a new

---

[5] Pound, *The Spirit of Romance* (New York: New Directions, n.d.—first published in 1910) 22.

[6] Pound, *Literary Essays*, 101.

movement, even if these poets seemed only dimly aware of where their experiments were leading.

> We also made ghostly visits, and the stair
> That knew us, found us again on the turn of it,
> And the sun-tanned, gracious and well-formed fingers
> Lift no latch of bent bronze, no Empire handle
> Twists for the knocker's fall; no voice to answer.
> A strange concierge, in place of the gouty-footed.
> Sceptic against all this one seeks the living,
> Stubborn against the facts.
>
> *Canto VII*

Pound could think of himself as a seeker like the troubadours of old, even if a seeker of more modem forms of poetic expression than theirs. His Imagism, for instance, promoted "free verse" as a kind of rhythmic liberation. Yet there was a further attraction for Pound that drew him to the troubadours: they moved about their limited world of Provence in the Middle Ages as easily as he moved about in the larger Anglo-French world of the twentieth century, with what he liked to call its double cultural capital of London and Paris. The troubadours moved from patron to patron through medieval Provence; Pound's migration from America to Europe, then from Italy to England to France and back to Italy, made him a peripatetic poet or wandering minstrel without a permanent home.

Pound had been a natural wanderer from his earliest days, traveling from Idaho, where he was born ("going east behind the first rotary snowplow" according to his own account in *Indiscretions*), to Philadelphia where he grew up, to Europe on family excursions, and finally to Europe to live, but keeping always on the move, settling first in Venice, then in London, then in Paris, then in Rapallo, then in Venice again: he was probably the most footloose great poet who ever lived, finding a home everywhere but never settling down anywhere for good. When Eliot met Pound in London in 1914, he observed that his fellow American was the most restless person he had ever known, always perched on the edge of his seat as if ready to move somewhere else.

So for Pound, with his interest in poetry and talent for writing it, his instinctive searching for origins and his natural wanderlust, it is not surprising that the Provençal troubadours were his first models, because they were inventors and they were itinerant. It is no more surprising that he took the troubadours as his real historical heroes than that he took Ulysses as his mythical Greek hero, because Ulysses was a wanderer, too, on the Mediterranean Sea between Ithaca and Troy. For that matter, he took Dante as his favorite poet, knowing that Dante wrote *The Divine Comedy* in exile from his native Florence. Pound also took the Anglo-Saxon poet of "The Seafarer" and the Chinese poets of *Cathay* as models, and later made Sextus Propertius, the strolling Latin poet, a mask for himself. When Pound projected as his prime alter ego the expatriate poet Hugh Selwyn Mauberley, he made him an American from "a half-savage country" who had moved to London just as Pound had done. And he was willing to seal "A Pact" with Walt Whitman, the American singer of the open road. Indeed, the emergent figure of the troubadour became so essential for Pound that it is to be found in all his poems, early and late, not least in the *Cantos*, his poetic odyssey and autobiography.

It has to be said, though, that if Pound chose to be a wandering troubadour, he was never rootless. "I have weathered the storm / I have beaten out my exile," he declared in an early poem, "The Rest," and he seemed to put down roots wherever he went, so that he could also be called a free-spirited American Agrarian, a follower of Jefferson in that respect as in others, who found nature as inspiring as men or women, and who made the natural environment of his poetry include the Schuylkill River in Philadelphia along with the Serpentine Pond in London, the Venetian Lagoon, and the Gulf of Tigullio at Rapallo. Pound found the natural world a constant source of inspiration wherever he chose to live, and so he could wander freely from place to place and be at home everywhere. His adaptability to place was part of what helped him become a modern troubadour. He loved the France of the medieval troubadours because he loved their poetry, and he took two long walking tours of the troubadour region of ancient Provence, one in 1912 and one in 1919, recording his journeys in long lyrics like "Provincia Deserta," and "Near Perigord," and short lyrics like "Langue d'Oc," all published in 1915, and later in the *Cantos:*

But to set here the roads of France,
     of Cahors, of Chalus,
     the inn low by the river's edge,
the poplars; to set here the roads of France
  Aubeterre, the quarried stone beyond Poitiers—
      —as seen against Sergeant Beaucher's
elegant profile
     and the tower on an almost triangular base
as seen from Santa Marta's in Tarascon
                         Canto LXXVI

Pound had put his affinity for the French countryside into prose in an essay of 1913 called "Troubadours—Their Sorts and Conditions," where he maintained that "a man may walk the hill roads and river roads from Limoges and Charente to Dordogne and Narbonne and learn a little, or more than a little, of what the country meant to the wandering singers."[7] It is clear that for Pound wandering was as much a part of a troubadour's life as singing, and it pleased his American sensibility that troubadours came from all social classes, not just from the noble class: "The poetry, as a whole, is the poetry of a democratic aristocracy, which swept into itself, or drew about it, every man with wit or a voice."[8] He respected these aristodemocratic troubadours for perfecting the complex poems of courtly love or *amour courtois* by means of experiments with verse technique, resulting in such new poetic forms as the sestina and the aube, both of which he practiced in English.

    Pound in many ways, then, began his poetic career as a troubadour; and a troubadour he remained, so that if there is a unifying presence in all of Pound's poetry, it is the figure of the modern troubadour, for proof of which we need only start naming those poems of Pound which could be properly called "troubadour songs." The list is a long one. It starts as early as 1908 with "Cino," in *A Lume Spento*, his first book of poems published in Venice, which combines love and wandering:

    I have sung women in three cities
    But it is all one.

---

[7] Pound, *Literary Essays*, 95.

[8] Pound, *The Spirit of Romance*, 39.

> I will sing of the white birds
> In the blue waters of heaven,
> The clouds that are spray to its sea.

The list of troubadour songs goes on with lines like "When I the dawn reflected in the west" in "Aube of the West Dawn. Venetian June" and "I go—my song upon the winds set free" in "To La Contessa Bianzafior (Cent. XIV)"—both from the *Quinzaine for this Yule,* Pound's first book of London poems published in 1908. *Personae* in 1909 contains "Na Audiart," with his portrait of the ideal lady of the love courts of Eleanor of Aquitaine:

> Or when the minstrel, tale half told
> Shall burst to lilting at the praise
>   "Audiart, Audiart . . ."
>
> Bertrans, master of his lays,
> Bertrans of Aultaforte thy praise
> Sets forth. . . .

mentioning Bertran even earlier than the famous "Sestina: Altaforte." Then there is "Li Bel Chasteus," or "The Beautiful Castle," which opens with a description of troubadour country, "That castle stands the highest in the land / Far seen and mighty" and the opening of "Aegypton" again brings together the wandering minstrel and the perfect lady of the *amour courtois*:

> I—even I—am he who knoweth the roads
> Thru the sky and the wind thereof is my body
>
> I have beheld the Lady of Life.
> I, even I, that fly with the swallows.

Pound wrote many poems other than the "Sestina: Altaforte" in the guise of a medieval French Troubadour, such as "Marvoil" for "Arnaut the less" (so called in comparison with the greater Arnaut Daniel) and "Piere Vidal Old," about the troubadour who goes mad for his love:

Behold me, Vidal, that was fool of fools!
Swift as the king wolf was I and as strong
When tall stags fled me through the alder brakes,
And every jongleur knew me in his song,
And the hounds fled and the deer fled
And none fled over-long.

We might even include "The Ballad of the Goodly Fere," for though Pound did not go so far as to make Christ a Troubadour, he did write a kind of latter-day Scottish ballad which portrayed Christ rather daringly as a roving figure, a fighter and a wanderer—indeed, Pound himself later jokingly called it his "Christ as a gangster" poem,

Oh we drank his Hale in the good red wine
When we last made company,
No capon priest was the Goodly Fere
But a man o' men was he.

Surely the good red wine with which they toasted Christ must have been French, and so was the capon that he forswore.

Pound identified himself most with Bertran de Born of all the troubadours, writing many poems about him, notably "The Planh for the Young English King" taken directly from Bertran's Provençal elegy for Prince Henry Plantagenet. It was the young Prince Henry on whose side Bertran fought against his father, King Henry II of England and much of France, making Bertran a "stirrer up of strife" whom Dante would place in the lowest circles of his Inferno. And in 1911, Pound published a whole book of *Canzoni*, all of them troubadour songs drawn from the Provençal poets: "Canzon: The Yearly Slain" and "Canzon: the Spear," "Canzon: To be sung beneath a Window," "Canzon: Of Incense," "Canzon: Of Angels," and "Canzon: The Vision."

Thus, by the time Pound had initiated the Imagist movement with *Ripostes* in 1912, he had written several volumes of poems based on the troubadours. His own style had been so well formed that he could translate "The Seafarer" from the Anglo-Saxon exactly as if it were another troubadour song:

Bitter breast-cares have I abided ,
Known on my keel many a care's hold,

> And dire sea-surge, and there I oft spent
> Narrow nightwatch nigh the ship's head
> While she tossed close to cliffs.

Here is what sounds like a troubadour poem from the Anglo-Saxon, because Pound's version of this Old English poem about a forlorn sailor on the wide sea is not far in content or rhythm from the landlocked lament of Bertran de Born as Pound portrays him in "Near Perigord":

> And ten years after, or twenty, as you will,
> Arnaut and Richard lodge beneath Chalus:
> The dull round towers encroaching on the field,
> The tents tight drawn, horses at tether
> Further and out of reach, the purple night,
> The crackling of small fires, the bannerets,
> The lazy leopards on the largest banner,
> Stray gleams on hanging mail, an armourer's torch-flare
> Melting on steel.

Pound's astonishingly diverse repertoire of troubadour songs was further enlarged to include the Chinese translations of *Cathay* in 1915, especially the wonderful "Exile's Letter,"

> We met, and travelled into Sen-Go,
> Through all the thirty-six folds of the turning and
> twisting waters,
> Into a valley of the thousand bright flowers,
> That was the first valley

where China becomes another Provence in Pound's handling of it, and the equally fine "Lament of the Frontier Guard":

> I climb the towers and towers
>   to watch out the barbarous land:
> Desolate castle, the sky, the wide desert.

which describes a Chinese landscape that resembles the Dordogne with its turrets and chateaux, while the singer resembles Bertran de Born in "Near Perigord":

> Let us say we see
> En Bertrans, a tower-room at Hautefort,
> Sunset, the ribbon-like road lies, in red cross-light,
> Southward toward Montaignac....

We are also not far from the poetry of *Langue d'Oc*, or Provençal, which Pound published in the same year, 1915, beginning with a fragmentary "Alba" or "Dawn Song," mentioned by Pound earlier in his essay, "Proença," in *The Spirit of Romance*, and there translated into prose:

> *When the nightingale cries to his mate, night and day, I am with my fair mistress amidst the flowers, until the watchman from the tower cries "Lover, arise, for I see the white light of the dawn, and the clear day."*

This same prose text in 1910 became one of his most stunning troubadour songs when Pound translated it poetically to open the collection *Langue d'Oc* in 1915:

Alba

> When the nightingale to his mate
> Sings day-long and night late
> My love and I keep state
> In bower,
> In flower,
> 'Till the watchman on the tower
> Cry:
>> "Up! Thou rascal, Rise,
>> I see the white
>>> Light
>>> And the night
>>>> Flies. "

The other poems of *Langue d'Oc* are also among his finest troubadour songs, especially the one beginning "O Plasmatour and true celestial light" with its refrain "O lord, how swift the night / And day comes on," which he attributes to Giraut de Bornelh of Excideuil.

It would be hard to omit any of the *Homage to Sextus Propertius* in 1917 from the list of Pound's troubadour songs, in particular number X, beginning "Light, light of my eyes, at an exceeding late hour I was wandering," which, like a troubadour *alba*, combines praise for his mistress Cynthia with the poet's late night stroll through the streets of Rome. And the poet he invented in *Hugh Selwyn Mauberley* in 1920, the culmination of his poetic work before the *Cantos*, must be regarded as another troubadour, even if living in a more decadent age. It could be said that when Pound wrote his "Sestina: Altaforte," he was trying to reincarnate Bertran de Born, but when he wrote *Mauberley*, he was trying to show that a modern troubadour could exist even in the midst of a "botched civilization."

And then there are the *Cantos*. With them, the list of troubadour songs becomes endless, starting with *Canto I* based on Homer's *Odyssey*, where Ulysses makes his journey to Hades, and *Canto II* derived from Ovid's *Metamorphoses*, where Dionysus is taken aboard a slave ship which he magically transforms into a vineyard, *Canto III* about the Cid, a Spanish warrior hero who rode against the Moors, and of course *Canto IV* about the troubadour Cabestan whose heart was served to his lady—"It is Cabestan's heart in the dish." *Canto VII* is about Eleanor of Aquitaine and also about Henry James, and the opening of *Canto XXVI* has lines depicting Pound in Venice, "And I came here in my young youth / and lay there under the crocodile." Certainly *Canto XXIX* concerning Sordello and his mistress Cunizza would have to be ranked as a troubadour song, and so would *Canto XLVII*, which reprises Ulysses' voyage to hell from the first Canto and then goes on to describe the lights in the sea at Rapallo which Pound often observed and arbitrarily linked with Aphrodite as well as the Virgin Mary, a sort of Italian *amour courtois*, and afterwards, it seems all of the great *Pisan Cantos* are troubadour songs, picturing the wandering American laid low, imprisoned for his outspokenness, and so, it could be argued, are the remaining *Rock-Drill* and *Thrones* and *Drafts & Fragments of Cantos CX-CXVII*. As one reads them through again and again, perhaps the *Cantos* form Pound's most extensive songs of a modern troubadour, since he is innovative and itinerant from beginning to end, just as were the medieval French troubadours Pound so much admired. It is enough to say that Pound's troubadour songs are to be found everywhere in his poetry, some of them directly translated from the Provençal but many generated from his own fertile imagination as if further examples of the *trobar clus*.

If Pound appears again and again from early to late in his poetry as a Modern Troubadour, it might be asked which of his poems best portray him in his favored role. The troubadour persona reappears many times in the *Cantos*, but the way is prepared by the creation of his fullest self-portrait, if an ironic one, in the eighteen sections of *Hugh Selwyn Mauberley: Life and Contacts*. Pound insisted that this poem was his farewell to London, which in a certain sense it was; he also called it a version of his *Homage to Sextus Propertius* for a later age, as it also was, and he said it was an attempt to condense the Henry James novel into poetry, still another way of looking at it. It can be read, too, as a history of the Imagist Decade, the second decade of the Twentieth Century, when Pound led the way to a new poetic style by means of the Imagist poem, dense with imagery, rhythmic variation, and multilingual rhymes. Clearly, *Mauberley* has many meanings, but finally it can be read as his persona of the modern troubadour, a failed poet in the eyes of the public but a successful poet to the cognoscenti. It is not out of the question to say that *Mauberley* is Pound's twentieth-century *trobar clus*.

Hugh Selwyn Mauberley qualifies as Pound's modern troubadour in several ways. For one, he is trying to "resuscitate the dead art / Of poetry; to maintain the 'sublime' / in the old sense"—a nod to the eloquence of the Greeks. Pound really believed that the Provençal troubadours had carried forward the Greek tradition of Western poetry, arguing in his essay on "The Tradition" in 1913 that "The two great lyric traditions which most concern us are that of the Melic poets and that of Provence."[9] Pound maintained that there was a refined craftsmanship in Classical Greek poetry which had been revived in Provençal troubadour poetry, for "both in Greece and in Provence the poetry attained its highest rhythmic and metrical brilliance at times when the arts of verse and music were most closely knit together." So it is significant that the "Envoi" which Pound attributes to Mauberley honors the singer of Edmund Waller's "Go, lovely rose," for music is closely allied to verse in that poem. Furthermore, it is a love poem with metaphysical overtones, as were the troubadour songs of the Provençal and

---

[9] Pound, *Literary Essays*, 91.

the Italian poets, a *trobar clus* in the modern style, as the *dolce stil nuove* of Dante had been a development of the earlier Provençal poem. Though Mauberley regards himself as a failure, he is not really a failure at all, since he has demonstrated with his "Envoi" that he can write exquisite love poetry of the sort which the troubadours might have admired, and which compares favorably with its model, the seventeenth century love song, "Go, lovely rose."

So Mauberley, though surrounded and eventually driven out by a decadent age, has justly earned the title of Twentieth-Century Troubadour. What about Pound? It is difficult to distinguish Pound from Mauberley, his ironic self portrait of the artist, but to any knowledgeable reader, the two are not the same. They differ most in that one (Mauberley) believes he is a failure and retreats to the distant South Pacific, whereas the other (Pound) simply goes from London to Paris and continues writing poetry and exerting influence on other writers and artists: we know that difference well. But what if Pound is seeking to communicate through his alter ego Mauberley that he is not a real failure after all, that if poetry such as "the age demanded" may be plastic and consumable, the poetry he has written is as durable as marble, or "the 'sculpture' of rhyme"? Pound was ingenious enough to dismiss his failed self for being over-refined, "bent resolutely on wringing lilies from the acorn," while his successful self parts company and goes on working toward a new Renaissance. The modern troubadour as Pound depicts him is an outward failure—Mr. Nixon advises him to "Give up verse, my boy, there's nothing in it"—but an inward artist to those who can appreciate his accomplishment, as Dante appreciated Arnaut Daniel, and as Eliot appreciated Pound. Self-critic though he is, Mauberley stands for an art that aspires to the highest degree of perfection:

> —Given that is his "fundamental passion"
> This urge to convey the relation
> Of eye-lid and cheek-bone
> By verbal manifestation;

The poet Mauberley who produces his cameo portrait of a lady in his "Envoi" admits that he has not achieved his ambition; he has not written poems worthy of the woman he loves, who seems indifferent to him, yet Pound the poet who created Mauberley does achieve his ambition, does "build her glories their longevity," and can say that even in death

> . . . our two dusts with Waller's shall be laid,
> Siftings on siftings in oblivion,
> Till change hath broken down
> All things save Beauty alone.

Pound the modern troubadour has tricked his own shadow, the fictional poet Mauberley, into permanence, and his twentieth-century *trobar clus* presents us with a self-portrait of the American expatriate, who has wandered to London and fallen in love with a beautiful, mysterious woman he idolizes, just as the Provençal troubadours did in their songs of courtly love. But as their poems have endured so will his. Pound's purported failure in *Hugh Selwyn Mauberley* was thus an ironic success, and the *trobar clus* of medieval Provence was winningly revived by a twentieth-century American poet.

5

POUND AND YEATS: THE POETICS OF
FRIENDSHIP

Pale hair that the moon has shaken
Down over the dark breast of the sea,
O magic her beauty has shaken
About the heart of me;
Out of you have I woven a dream
That shall walk in the lonely vale
Betwixt the high hill and the low hill,
Until the pale stream
Of the souls of men quench and grow still.

A reader encountering this brief lyric, entitled "He speaks to the moonlight concerning the Beloved," in a slim volume called *Exultations* published in London in 1909, might have imagined he was reading a poem by William Butler Yeats that had somehow strayed from its Irish author's third volume, *The Wind Among the Reeds*, published ten years earlier, in 1899. But in fact he would have been reading the fourth volume of poems by a young American recently arrived in London, whose ambition was to start a new literary Renaissance, and whose strategy for storming the heights of Parnassus was to imitate, translate, parody, or if need be plagiarize every good poet, ancient or modern, that he could find. "Be influenced by as many great artists as you can" was his advice to other poets, "but have the decency either to acknowledge the debt outright, or to try to conceal it."[1] He would soon become much more adept at concealing his debts, but at the time Ezra Pound came to London, he declared openly that there was just one poet writing in English who was worthy of a younger poet's study, and that was Yeats.

Pound had arrived in London in 1908, fresh from Venice, where he had published his first volume of poems, with its title borrowed from Dante, *A Lume Spento* ("With Tapers Quenched," a phrase from Canto III of the *Purgatorio*, signifying burial without the rites of the church), and with a note to

---

[1] Pound, "A Retrospect," 5.

one of the poems saying that its mood had been appropriated from "Mr. Yeats in his 'Celtic Twilight,'" a mood of separation between a "corporal" self and an "aetherial" self. The poem was called "La Fraisne, or The Ash Tree," and the debt to Yeats was obvious enough:

> I have put aside all folly and grief.
> I wrapped my tears in an ellum leaf
> And left them under a stone . . .

Pound had sent a copy of this first book to Yeats and was pleased to hear that Yeats liked it: "W. B. Yeats applies the adjective 'charming,'" he wrote to William Carlos Williams in 1908, and in the following year he was able to add, "I have been praised by the greatest living poet."[2] By then, Pound had succeeded in meeting Yeats, and a friendship had begun between the older poet and the younger poet that blossomed into one of the most fruitful in modern letters. The introducer had been Olivia Shakespear, a lawyer's wife and a writer herself (and, as we now know, Yeats's mistress for a time), who with her daughter Dorothy had attended Pound's lectures in 1909, and had taken him to one of Yeats's Monday evenings, in his flat at 18 Woburn Buildings, near Russell Square. It is remarkable how quickly their friendship ripened, considering that in 1910, in *The Green Helmet and Other Poems*, Yeats issued a warning to any poet who might dare to follow him too closely, in "To a Poet, who would have me Praise certain Bad Poets, Imitators of His and Mine":

> You say, as I have often given tongue
> In praise of what another's said or sung,
> 'Twere politic to do the like by these;
> But was there ever dog that praised his fleas?

Although Yeats was addressing his friend George Russell (AE), and the imitators were young Irish poets, it was Pound's good luck not to be taken for one of the "fleas."

But while it was Pound who initiated the friendship, it was Yeats who, more and more in the years that followed their first meeting, sought the advice of the younger poet, and in a few years they became active collaborators, with Yeats

---

[2] Pound, *Letters*, 7-8.

depending on Pound as much as Pound had once depended on Yeats. The poetics of their friendship overcame all barriers, and allowed an established Irish poet in his mid-forties and an aspiring American poet in his mid-twenties to influence each other, as they also influenced others, and so to shape a new poetic style in English. Yeats was moving from the softness of his Celtic Twilight period to the hardness of *Responsibilities*, which when it appeared in 1914 Pound hailed as "The Later Yeats," while Pound was transforming himself from an imitator to a critic and parodist of the Early Yeats, who in 1915 in his volume *Lustra* produced his own inimitable "The Lake Isle" in answer to Yeats's well-known "The Lake Isle of Innisfree":

> O God, O Venus, O Mercury, patron of thieves,
> Give me in due time, I beseech you, a little tobacco-shop,
> With the little bright boxes
>   piled up neatly upon the shelves
> And the loose fragrant cavendish
>   and the shag,
> And the bright Virginia
>   loose under the bright glass cases,
> And a pair of scales not too greasy,
> And the whores dropping in for a word or two in passing,
> For a flip word, and to tidy their hair a bit.

> O God, O Venus, O Mercury, patron of thieves,
> Lend me a little tobacco-shop,
>   or install me in any profession
> Save this damn'd profession of writing,
>   where one needs one's brains all the time.

Except for its title, there is nothing imitative of Yeats in this later poem; in fact, its style is quite opposite to that of the original "Innisfree" and deliberately plays off the gossipy intimacy of a gathering place in the city against the idyllic solitude of nature. Pound's flippant, irreverent invocation of the gods as "patron[s] of thieves" is maintained until the final lines, when he suddenly becomes serious and changes the scene from a tobacco shop to a writer's study and directs the satire at himself and his own artistic endeavor. We are far from Innisfree, certainly, but not so far from other poems Yeats had written when he was changing his style from romantic to modern, making the transition that Pound of all readers was most alert to, as in one of the poems of *The Green Helmet* in 1910:

> All things can tempt me from this craft of verse;
> One time it was a woman's face, or worse—
> The seeming needs of my fool-driven land;
> Now nothing but comes readier to the hand
> Than this accustomed toil. When I was young,
> I had not given a penny for a song
> Did not the poet sing it with such airs
> That one believed he had a sword upstairs;
> Yet would be now, could I but have my wish,
> Colder and dumber and deafer than a fish.

What Pound's parody of "Innisfree" shows, beneath its air of ironic detachment, is a seriousness about the profession of poet amounting to despair, over the impossible demands it makes on him, linking him with Yeats in a way that is characteristically modern—the poet's self-criticism of his own art. By the time they wrote major poems in the new style, Yeats in *The Wild Swans at Coole* (1919) and Pound in *Homage to Sextus Propertius* (1919) and *Hugh Selwyn Mauberley* (1920), the figure of the poet as a failed hero and disillusioned idealist, struggling to create beauty despite the destructive materialistic tendencies of the age, had become a central subject for both poets. It was their serious view of literature as the most exacting of arts, "this craft of verse," "this damn'd profession of writing," that brought them together at a crucial period in each poet's development and caused them to produce the series of tragic-ironic self-portraits of the artist that placed them in the vanguard of modern poets. In a famous passage in his prose work *Per Amica Silentia Lunae*, in 1917, Yeats wrote, "We make out of the quarrel with others, rhetoric, but of the quarrel with ourselves, poetry," and he went on to say that "the other self, the anti-self or the antithetical self, as one may choose to name it, comes but to those who are no longer deceived, whose passion is reality." And Pound in "A Retrospect," in 1918, said that "Mr. Yeats has once and for all stripped English poetry of its perdamnable rhetoric. He has boiled away all that is not poetic." Much later, in 1937, Pound would write that in the years from 1908 to 1914, "I was learning how Yeats did it," and what he learned was "mostly negative, i.e., he has stripped English poetry of many of its faults." Remarkably enough, Yeats credited Pound with doing much the same for him, when, at a dinner given in his honor by *Poetry* magazine in Chicago in 1914, he summed up what Pound had done for him in the five years of their friendship:

> We rebelled against rhetoric, and now there is a group of younger poets who dare to call us rhetorical. When I returned to London from Ireland, I had a young man go over all my work to eliminate the abstract. This was an American poet, Ezra Pound.[3]

Much of what Yeats and Pound exchanged in the years of their closest association, from 1909 to 1916, was frankly critical, a mutual effort to rid themselves of conventional habits of expression, to write more honestly, even to write of their own faults without embarrassment. Pound taught Yeats fencing to improve his health, and they engaged in verbal fencing matches to improve their style. As Yeats said in his remarks at the *Poetry* banquet in 1914, "The whole movement of poetry is toward pictures, sensuous images, away from rhetoric, from the abstract, toward humility." It seems that together Yeats and Pound taught each other as much about how *not* to write poetry as how to write it, taking their pleasure in what was hardest to do, making their subject the pain of artistic endeavor in the pursuit of perfection. Yeats wrote in *The Green Helmet* in 1910:

> The fascination of what's difficult
> Has dried the sap out of my veins, and rent
> Spontaneous joy and natural content
> Out of my heart . . ..

And Pound wrote in *Lustra* in 1915:

---

[3] An account of Yeats's speech appeared in the April 1914 issue of *Poetry* and is reprinted in Vol. 2 of *The Uncollected Prose of W. B. Yeats*, ed. John P. Frayne and Colton Johnson (New York, 1975) 412-14.

Go, my songs, seek your praise from the young
and from the intolerant,
Move among the lovers of perfection alone.
Seek ever to stand in the hard Sophoclean light
And take your wounds from it gladly.

Pound had come to Yeats as a younger admirer, ready to learn from an older poet; Yeats seemed to regard him at once as one of the young and intolerant from whom he too could learn. Early in 1910, Pound wrote to his mother of Yeats, "He is the only living man whose work has anything more than temporary interest—possible exceptions on the continent," and later that year, in his preface to *The Spirit of Romance,* he had already placed Yeats among the immortals, saying, "What we need is a literary scholarship that will weigh Theocritus and Yeats with one balance." Yeats, for his part, wrote to Lady Gregory at the end of 1910 about "this queer creature Ezra Pound, who has become really a great authority on the troubadours," and said with evident admiration that he "has, I think, got closer to the right sort of music for poetry than Mrs. Emery [the actress Florence Farr, adept at reading poetry aloud]—it is more definitely music with strongly marked time and yet it is effective speech." But Yeats went on, in a more critical vein, "However, he cannot sing, as he has no voice. It is like something on a very bad phonograph."[4] Though Pound and Yeats often read aloud to each other, privately each found fault with the other's vocal style, as we can gather from Pound's recollection:

> Years ago Yeats was struggling with my rhythms and saying they wouldn't do. I got him to read a little Burns aloud, telling him he cd. read no cadence but his own. ... I had a half hour of unmitigated glee in hearing "Say ye bonnie Alexander" and "The Birks O' Aberfeldy" keened, wailed with infinite difficulty and many

---

[4] *The Letters of William Butler Yeats*, ed. Allen Wade (New York, 1955), 543.

pauses and restarts to *The Wind Among the Reeds*.[5]

If they admired the music in each other's poetry, it was for the way it was written rather than the way it was read.

In 1911, Yeats met Pound in Paris for the first of several excursions they took together on the Continent. They went to the Sorbonne, to Versailles, and to Notre Dame, and Yeats's response to the cathedral was memorably recorded much later in *Canto LXXXIII:*

> and Uncle William dawdling around Notre Dame
> in search of whatever
>   paused to admire the symbol
> with Notre Dame standing inside it

In 1912, the relation between them became more professional, when Pound, as foreign editor of the newly founded *Poetry* magazine in Chicago, asked Yeats to submit some poems. Yeats obliged with five of his new poems, "The Realists," "The Mountain Tomb," "To a Child Dancing upon the Shore," "A Memory of Youth," and "Fallen Majesty." Pound accepted them, but made slight changes in the wording of three of the poems before sending them off to Harriet Monroe for publication. He deleted three superfluous words ("as it were") from "Fallen Majesty," changed an "or" to a grammatically preferable "nor" in "The Mountain Tomb," and corrected Yeats's grammar again in "To a Child Dancing upon the Shore" by substituting "him" for "he." When he showed these fairly trivial but justifiable changes to Yeats, their friendship was sorely tested, since Yeats was offended and took them all back for further revision. In the end, however, Yeats accepted Pound's deletion in one poem and rewrote the other two, retitling one of them "To a Child Dancing in the Wind." When Pound finally sent the poems to Chicago, he told Harriet Monroe that "peace reigns on Parnassus."[6] This incident gives us the only documentation that has turned up so far of what

---

[5] Pound, *Letters*, 180.

[6] Richard Ellmann, "Ez and Old Billyum," in *Eminent Domain: Yeats Among Wilde, Joyce, Pound, Eliot and Auden* (New York, 1967) 67.

Pound did to improve Yeats's poetry. It was practical criticism of the sort he offered to many of his contemporaries. What seems exceptional is that he offered it as readily to an older, established poet as he did to younger writers like Joyce and Eliot and Hemingway. Yeats may have bristled at first, but eventually he came to respect Pound's editorial judgment so much that he asked Pound to become his private secretary. As Yeats wrote to his father in the summer of 1913:

> Next winter I am taking a secretary though I shrink from the expense, believing that I shall be able to bear the expense because I shall be able to write. When my sec comes at the end of October you will find me a better correspondent as he will answer business letters.[7]

That Pound served as much more than a stenographer for Yeats is clear from another letter Yeats wrote the same year to Lady Gregory:

> My digestion has got rather queer again, a result of sitting up late with Ezra and Sturge Moore and some light wine while the talk ran. However, the criticism I got from them has given me new life and I have made that Tara poem [probably "The Two Kings," published in *Poetry* in 1913 and *Responsibilities* in 1914] a new thing and am writing with new confidence having got Milton off my back. Ezra is the best critic of the two. He is full of the middle ages and helps me get back to the definite and concrete and away from modern abstractions. To talk over a poem with him is like getting you to put a sentence into dialect. All becomes clear and natural.[8]

In order to seclude themselves for serious work, Yeats invited Pound to spend the winter with him at a cottage he had rented near London, and in November 1913 the two poets betook

---

[7] Yeats, *Letters*, 584.

[8] Quoted by Ellmann, 66.

themselves to Stone Cottage, Coleman's Hatch, in the Ashdown Forest of Sussex. Pound's view of the enterprise was not very optimistic, as he wrote to his mother before going there: "My stay in Stone Cottage will not be in the least profitable. I detest the country. Yeats will amuse me part of the time and bore me to death with psychical research the rest. I regard the visit as a duty to posterity."[9] However, the experience seems to have cemented the friendship between the two poets, for Pound wrote in December to William Carlos Williams: "Yeats is much finer *intime* than seen spasmodically in the midst of a whirl. We are both, I think, very contented in Sussex."[10]

Pound had formed another valuable literary friendship with Ford Madox Ford, the novelist and editor of the *English Review*, whom he saw often in London, and Ford (then Hueffer) invited the two poets over to his cottage at Slough for a week in late December (1913). Of this sojourn Pound wrote one of his most amusing letters to his mother, which reads in part:

> Am down here for a week with the Hueffers in a dingy old cottage that belonged to Milton. F.M.H. and I being the two people who couldn't be in the least impressed by the fact, makes it a bit more ironical....
> Yeats reading to me up till late Sat. evening,
>   etc ....
> Have written about 20 new poems.
> 3 days later:
> Impossible to get any writing done here. Atmosphere too literary.
> 3 "Kreators" all in one ancient cottage is a bit thick.[11]

While Yeats was correlating Lady Gregory's collection of Irish myths and folklore with the folklore and religion of other countries during part of this time, he and Pound were writing poems, and Pound was editing *Des Imagistes*, the first anthology of Imagist poems. Yeats suggested to Pound that he

---

[9] Pound, *Letters*, 25.

[10] Pound, *Letters*, 27

[11] Pound, *Letters*, 28.

get in touch with a promising young Irish author then living in Trieste, as a result of which Pound wrote to James Joyce for the first time, asking to see some of his work. But before Joyce had time to reply, Yeats had unearthed a poem from Joyce's *Chamber Music* called "I Hear an Army Charging" and showed it to Pound. Pound liked it so much that he wrote again to ask Joyce for permission to include the poem in *Des Imagistes*, and Joyce obliged. This first communication between Joyce and Pound was of crucial importance to Joyce's career, since it led to the serial publication of *A Portrait of the Artist as a Young Man* in the *Egoist* magazine in 1914, when Pound was serving as one of the editors, and in time to serial publication of *Ulysses*, beginning in 1918 in *The Little Review*, for which Pound was then foreign editor. Thus Yeats was able to help both Pound and Joyce, and he was especially generous with Pound when, that same winter at Stone Cottage, he received a prize of fifty pounds from *Poetry* for "The Grey Rock," a poem Pound had sent in for him, and publicly requested Harriet Monroe to give forty pounds of it to Pound, "because," as he said in his open letter to her, "although I do not really like with my whole soul the metrical experiments he has made for you, I think those experiments show a vigorous creative mind."[12] Pound commemorated Yeats's generous act by buying a new typewriter "of great delicacy," along with some statues from his sculptor friend, Henri Gaudier-Brzeska.

It was in January of 1914 that Yeats and Pound joined other poets in London for a dinner in honor of the older English poet, Wilfred Scawen Blunt, at which Pound read a verse tribute and presented a statue by Gaudier, and Yeats made a short speech in praise of Blunt, in the course of which he spoke of the changes then occurring in English poetry, declaring that "we are now at the end of Victorian romance—completely at an end. . . . Every year some part of my poetical machinery suddenly becomes of no use. As the tide of romance recedes I am driven back simply on myself and my thoughts in actual life."[13] He spoke of younger poets who were in rebellion against romanticism, especially of Ezra Pound, who, he said, "has a

---

[12] Yeats, *Letters*, 585.

[13] Excerpts from Yeats's speech were quoted in the *Egoist*, February 2, 1914, 57.

desire personally to insult the world" (with Pound no doubt smiling in the audience). Two months later, at the *Poetry* banquet in Chicago, Yeats was more complimentary of Pound, saying, "Much of his work is experimental; his work will come slowly, he will make many an experiment before he comes into his own," and then reading two of Pound's poems that he believed were "of permanent value," "The Ballad of the Goodly Fere" and "The Return." He called "The Return" "the most beautiful poem that has been written in the free form, one of the few in which I find real organic rhythm. A great many poets use *vers libre* because they think it is easier to write than rhymed verse, but it is much more difficult."

Pound's poem had appeared in 1912 in *Ripostes*, the seventh collection of his poems, the one in which his new Imagist style had become most evident. For Yeats, "The Return" was the poem he continued to admire the most of all Pound's work, not only for its masterful use of free verse, but for its vision of the ancient gods returning to earth. Yeats used it many years later in the preface of the revised edition of *A Vision*, and he said in 1929, in *A Packet for Ezra Pound*, after explaining how his wife's automatic writing had brought him the vision of history as a complex interaction of cones and gyres:

> You will hate these generalities, Ezra, which are themselves, it may be, of the past— the abstract sky—yet you have written "The Return," and though you but announce in it some change of style, perhaps, in book and picture it gives me better words than my own.[14]

Yeats's use of Pound's poem may seem remarkable, when he had written so many fine visionary poems himself, but it does bear a more than superficial resemblance to his own poem, "The Magi," written during the period of Yeats's closest association with Pound and published in 1914 in *Poetry*. Pound praised it for its "quality of hard light" and quoted it as an example of Imagism by a poet who was not an Imagist, maintaining that "a

---

[14] Yeats, *A Vision*, reissued with the author's final revisions (New York, 1966) 29.

passage of imagisme may occur in a poem not otherwise imagiste" and indicating that Yeats's poetry was in key with the new poetic style. Setting the poems side by side shows how much they have in common:

The Return

See, they return; ah, see the tentative
        Movements, and the slow feet,
        The trouble in the pace and the uncertain
        Wavering!

See, they return, one, and by one,
With fear, as half-awakened;
As if the snow should hesitate
And murmur in the wind,
           and half turn back;
These were the "Wing'd-with-Awe,"
        Inviolable.

Gods of the winged shoe!
With them the silver hounds,
           sniffing the trace of air!

Haie! Haie!
        These were the swift to harry;
        These the keen-scented;
        These were the souls of blood.

        Slow on the leash,
           pallid the leash-men!

The Magi

Now as at all times I can see in the mind's eye,
In their stiff, painted clothes, the pale unsatisfied ones
Appear and disappear in the blue depth of the sky
With all their ancient faces like rain-beaten stones,
And all their helms of silver hovering side by side,
And all their eyes still fixed, hoping to find once more,

> Being by Calvary's turbulence unsatisfied,
> The uncontrollable mystery on the bestial floor.

Different as these poems are in their rhythms and sounds, they display a marked similarity of imagery and tone, for both depict a group of superhuman figures seen as ominous but thrilling apparitions, described as "troubled" and "unsatisfied" in their bearing, as if they expected some momentous change and were impatient for it to take place. Both poems are prophetic, and the prophecies are dark although at the same time alluring. The key color word in both is "silver," which blends with the stormy atmosphere to give a tone of coldness and harshness to the apparitions. What these gods and Magi appear to be foretelling is a time of adversity, perhaps the end of Christian civilization and the beginning of another epoch, with supernatural forces controlling events more than men.

Probably no two poems by Yeats or Pound are closer than these short lyrics, and the praise each gave to the other's poem would indicate the affinity they felt. Yeats's poem appeared in the May 1914 issue of *Poetry*, along with a number of his poems that were published at the same time in *Responsibilities*, notably "To A Friend Whose Work Has Come to Nothing," "The Peacock," and "A Coat," all poems exemplary of the change in Yeats's style from early to later. Pound had been the first to speak of "The Later Yeats," giving that title to his review of *Responsibilities* in the same issue of *Poetry*, and calling Yeats "so assuredly immortal that there is no need for him to recast his style to suit our winds of doctrine," but noting "a manifestly new note in his later work" that younger poets "might do worse than attend to." Pound said the new note had become audible as early as 1910 in *The Green Helmet*, and "since that time, one has felt his work becoming gaunter, seeking a new hardness of outline." Besides praising "The Magi" and "A Coat," he spoke highly of "the poems on the Irish gallery," meaning "September, 1913" and others composed by Yeats in his indignation over the failure of Ireland to raise a public subscription for a gallery in Dublin to house Hugh Lane's collection of French Impressionist paintings. Pound commented approvingly that "we find this author certainly at *prise* with things as they are and no longer romantically Celtic."

It is likely that Yeats composed all these poems Pound admired while the two were staying at Stone Cottage in the winter of 1913-14. We may conclude this from their publication soon afterward in *Poetry*, and also from a much later source of evidence, Pound's *Pisan Cantos*, where "The Peacock" is quoted as part of Pound's evocation of the ancient cottage, and the creative interaction of the two poets within it, for which the peacock may well have been a symbol:

The Peacock

> What's riches to him
> That has made a great peacock
> With the pride of his eye?
> The wind-beaten, stone-grey,
> And desolate Three Rock
> Would nourish his whim.
> Live he or die
> Amid wet rocks and heather,
> His ghost will be gay
> Adding feather to feather
> For the pride of his eye.

Pound colors the scene in his memory, and adds a note of hilarity to the composition of the poem, doubtless unnoticed by Yeats in the fervor of his invention:

> so that I recalled the noise in the chimney
> as it were the wind in the chimney
> but was in reality Uncle William
> downstairs composing
> that had made a great Peeeeacock
> in the proide ov his oiye
>
> proide ov his oy-ee
> as indeed he had, and perdurable
>
> a great peacock aere perennius
> or as in the advice to the young man to
> breed and get married (or not)
> as you choose to regard it
>
> at Stone Cottage in Sussex by the waste moor
> (or whatever) and the holly bush

who would not eat ham for dinner
because peasants eat ham for dinner
despite the excellent quality
and the pleasure of having it hot.

well those days are gone forever
and the traveling rug with the coon-skin tabs
and his hearing nearly all Wordsworth
for the sake of his conscience but
preferring Ennemosor on Witches

did we ever get to the end of Doughty:
The Dawn in Britain?
perhaps not
Summons withdrawn, sir.)
Canto LXXXIII

It was in April of 1914 that Pound married Olivia Shakespear's daughter Dorothy, and Yeats told his father in New York that he must hurry home for the wedding. The Pounds chose to honeymoon in Stone Cottage, and the following winter Yeats, who was past fifty but still a bachelor, came to join them there. In all, the poets spent three highly productive winters together, Pound publishing in 1915 his first collection of Chinese translations, *Cathay*, and an anthology of new poems by contemporary poets, *The Catholic Anthology*, which included a few poems by T. S. Eliot, a recent discovery of Pound's, as well as Yeats's poem, "The Scholars." Yeats invited Pound to edit a selection of passages from the letters of his father, John Butler Yeats, for the Cuala Press in Dublin run by Yeats's sisters, and Pound was glad to oblige, since he liked to quote phrases from the elder Yeats's letters in his own letters and essays. Yeats explained in one of his letters his reason for asking Pound to do it: "I thought he would make the selection better than I should. I am almost too familiar with the thought, and also that his approval, representing as he does the most aggressive contemporary school of the young, would be of greater value than my approval, which would seem perhaps but family feeling."[15] Pound was also spending much of his time deciphering the manuscripts of Ernest Fenollosa, and finishing

---

[15] Yeats, *Letters*, 606-07.

his translation of Japanese Noh plays. In 1916, the Cuala Press published *Certain Noble Plays of Japan: From the Manuscripts of Ernest Fenollosa, Chosen and Finished by Ezra Pound*, with an introduction by Yeats. Yeats gave as his reason for including these Oriental dramas in a normally Irish series that "I have asked Mr. Pound for these beautiful plays because I think they will help me to explain a certain possibility of the Irish dramatic movement." Yeats had found in Pound's Noh plays a new way of conceiving of theater with the actors wearing masks, and he wrote a play about his mythical Irish hero Cuchulain on the model of the Noh. In introducing it, Yeats claimed that "I have invented a form of drama distinguished, indirect and symbolic, and having no need of a mob or press to pay its way—an aristocratic form." This play was *At the Hawk's Well*, the first of Yeats's plays for dancers and masks, and instead of being staged at the Abbey Theatre in Dublin, as his earlier plays had been, it was played in a London drawing room to an invited audience. Yeats conceded that popular drama must be realistic, but since he preferred poetic drama, he saw in the Japanese court theater a new potentiality: "In the studio and in the drawing-room we can found a true theatre of beauty."

Pound not only supplied the model for this new drama of Yeats, but he found a Japanese dancer to act in it, helped to stage the play at Lady Cunard's house in London, and even had something to do with the guest list. We know from one member of the audience, T. S. Eliot, what effect the play had on him:

> Yeats was well-known, of course; but to me, at least, Yeats did not appear, until after 1917, to be anything but a minor survivor of the '90's. (After that date, I saw him very differently. I remember clearly my impression of the first performance of *The Hawk's Well* in a London drawing room, with a celebrated Japanese dancer in the role of the hawk, to which Pound took me. And thereafter one saw Yeats rather as a more eminent contemporary than as an elder from whom one could learn.)[16]

---

[16] Eliot, "Ezra Pound (1946)," 25.

Pound spoke of the play as "new Theatre, or theatreless drama," and applauded Yeats's departure from the conventional stage. Yeats was satisfied enough with the result of his experiment to write another Cuchulain play along the same lines, *The Only Jealousy of Emer*, which he produced in 1919.

But poetry was still Yeats's main interest, as it was Pound's, and in 1917 Pound became foreign editor of *The Little Review* and provided a new outlet for their work. A large group of Yeats's poems appeared in the June 1917 issue of the magazine, including "The Wild Swans at Coole," which would become the title poem of his next collection, and such memorable poems about his still unrequited love for Maud Gonne as "A Deep-Sworn Vow" and "Broken Dreams." In *The Little Review*, Yeats was in the company of the best of the younger generation, Joyce and Eliot as well as Pound, and he clearly belonged with them. When finally he married in October 1917, at the age of 52, he took as his wife Georgie Hyde-Lees, only 24, the close friend and cousin-in-law of Dorothy Shakespear Pound, and fittingly, Ezra was his best man. Yeats trusted Pound with the arrangements for the wedding, but when he asked him to send a telegram to Lady Gregory at Coole Park, he stipulated that the message should be "*not* one that will be talked about in Gort for the next generation."

In 1918, Pound published a book of essays called *Pavannes and Divisions*, which contained "A Retrospect," his fullest summary of the changes that had taken place in English poetry in the previous decade. He spoke especially of the difference Imagism had made in realistic presentation, economy of language, and rhythmical variety, but used Yeats as his chief example of the new spare style, saying, "He has become a classic in his own lifetime and *nel mezzo del cammin*. He has made our poetic idiom a thing pliable, a speech without inversions," and testified to "the lines of Yeats that ring in my head and in the heads of all young men of my time who care for poetry." In 1919, Yeats published *The Wild Swans at Coole*, with the theme that the heart grows old, and that

> The living beauty is for younger men:
> We cannot pay its tribute of wild tears.

In this book, Yeats made poetic capital of the painful contrast between his aging body and his youthful mind, casting himself

as "A weather-worn, marble triton / Among the streams." But
when he received the Nobel Prize in 1923, Yeats looked at the
medal, which depicted a young poet listening to the Muse, and
reflected, "I was goodlooking once like that young man, but my
unpracticed verse was full of infirmity, my Muse old as it were;
and now I am old and rheumatic, and nothing to look at, but my
Muse is young."[17] How he had transformed his Old Muse into a
Young Muse is partly explained in a note appended, in 1924, to
his essay "Blake's illustrations to Dante," where he says that
"some seven or eight years ago I asked my friend Mr. Ezra
Pound to point out everything in the language of my poems that
he thought an abstraction, and I learned from him how much
further the movement against abstraction had gone than my
generation had thought possible."[18]

Pound was now writing his longer poems about poets,
Homage to Sextus Propertius (1919) and *Hugh Selwyn Mauberley* (1920), in which he cast himself in a similar, prematurely
aging role, as a neglected poet who thinks he will

> have, doubtless, a boom after my funeral,
> Seeing that long standing increases all things
> Regardless of quality,

and who writes his own mock-epitaph:

> He passed from men's memory in *l'an trentuniesme*
> *De son eage*; the case presents
> No adjunct to the Muses's diadem.

The figure of the poet as a self-admitted failure, "out of key
with his time," who

> strove to resuscitate the dead art
> Of poetry: to maintain "the sublime"
> In the old sense.

bears a strong resemblance to the poet as Yeats was depicting
him at that time:

---

[17] "The Bounty of Sweden," in *The Autobiography of William Butler Yeats*
(New York: Doubleday Anchor Books, 1958) 365.
[18] Yeats, *Essays and Introductions* (New York, 1961) 145.

> Whether we have chosen chisel, pen or brush,
> We are but critics, or but half create,
> Timid, entangled, empty and abashed,
> Lacking the countenance of our friends.
> ("Ego Dominus Tuus," in *The Wild Swans at Coole*)

In fact, some of the sections of Pound's *Mauberley* are a poetic condensation of certain passages in Yeats's *Autobiography*, for in the section titled "The Tragic Generation," Yeats gave an account of the downfall of his fellow-poets in the Rhymers' Club, some of whom Pound describes poetically: "how Johnson (Lionel) died / By falling from a high stool in a pub" and "Dowson found harlots cheaper than hotels." Yeats had survived the weaknesses of his generation of poets by singular devotion to his art and had learned to make great poetry out of human frailty: "A poet writes always of his personal life, in his finest work out of its tragedy," he said in 1937 in "A General Introduction for My Work." And Pound learned from Yeats's experience as well as his own to view the poet as a man whose gift intensifies the pain of human existence even as it shapes it into art:

> Beneath the sagging roof
> The stylist has taken shelter,
> Unpaid, uncelebrated,
> At last from the world's welter.
> (*Hugh Selwyn Mauberley*, X)

What Pound liked to refer to as the "hardness" of the new poetic style was not simply a sharper imagery but the feeling of pain endured, and poetry, for both Yeats and Pound, was a discipline of the emotions to endure the pain and suffering that are a necessary part of life, a willingness to face the worst life could offer without sentimentality or self-delusion:

> The rhetorician would deceive his neighbours,
> The sentimentalist himself; while art
> Is but a vision of reality.
> ("Ego Dominus Tuus")

After 1920, Yeats and Pound saw each other much less frequently, for Yeats was increasingly occupied with Irish politics, and Pound moved from London to Paris and on to Rapallo. Their paths met only when Yeats traveled to Italy to see Pound, as he did in 1924, when the two poets toured Sicily together, Yeats being enchanted with the Byzantine mosaics he saw at Monreale and in the Palatine Chapel in Palermo, and Pound recalling later that Yeats asked him to speak some poetry aloud in the old Greek amphitheatre at Syracuse, to which he responded by quoting a line from Homer in Greek. It was in 1928 that Pound published two new Yeats poems in his magazine, *Exile*, along with his own *Canto XXIII*. Yeats's poems were "Sailing to Byzantium" and "Blood and the Moon." Yeats's Byzantium imagery owed something to his tour of Sicily with Pound:

> O sages standing in God's holy fire,
> As in the gold mosaic of a wall...

and when Yeats later published his "Crazy Jane" cycle in *The Winding Stair and Other Poems* in 1933, he made his only direct borrowing from Pound. Two lines of "Those Dancing Days are Gone" read:

> I carry the sun in a golden cup,
> The moon in a silver bag.

In a note to these lines, Yeats wrote, "'The sun in a golden cup' . . . though not 'The moon in a silver bag' is a quotation from the last of Mr. Ezra Pound's *Cantos*" (actually, *Canto XXIII*). Yeats was always troubled by Pound's *Cantos*, though he found much to admire in them, and he continued to regard Pound as one of the artists most sensitive to the age, an accurate recorder of the time Yeats himself envisioned, that of the "widening gyre" of European civilization, when "mere anarchy is loosed upon the world." In a note to his play, *Fighting the Waves*, published in 1934 in a collection called *Wheels and Butterflies*, Yeats speculated that "Europe is changing its philosophy" and saw it reflected especially in the later work of Pound and Joyce and Virginia Woolf:

> Certain typical books—*Ulysses*, Mrs. Virginia
> Woolf's *The Waves*, Mr. Ezra Pound's *Draft of*
> *XXX Cantos*—suggest a philosophy like that of

the Samkara school of ancient India, mental and
physical objects alike material, a deluge of experience breaking over us and within us, melting
limits whether of line or tint; man no hard bright
mirror dawdling by the dry sticks of a hedge, but
a swimmer, or rather the waves themselves.[19]

In this view, Yeats saw Pound as one of the writers who gave
voice to the fragmentation and disunity of the age, which Yeats
himself mirrored in *A Vision* and later poems, but with the
difference that he reacted strongly against them, countering
them in his poetry, posing a unity of art against the disunity of
the world. The difference is well illustrated by a comparison of
two of their poems written at this time, "Sailing to Byzantium"
and *Canto XXIII*. To do so is rather like comparing a painting
with a mosaic, since Yeats's poem expresses a desire to
transcend earthly existence, in perfectly controlled stanzas,
while Pound's expresses a similar desire in lyric fragments of
free verse. It could be said that the themes of the two poets
continued to run parallel, while their forms increasingly
diverged.

Yeats recognized how complementary the two poets
were, as men and as artists, when he wrote *A Packet for Ezra
Pound* in 1929. By then, he was in his mid-sixties, and had
come to Italy with his wife and children for his health. After
battling alone for some years in the senate of the new Irish Free
State, Yeats wrote to Olivia Shakespear in 1928: "I am tired, I
want nothing but the sea-shore and the palms and Ezra to
quarrel with, and the Rapallo cats to feed after nightfall."[20] He
found Rapallo "an indescribably lovely place" to live, and as for
company, he said, "I shall not lack conversation. Ezra Pound,
whose art is the opposite of mine, whose criticism commends
what I most condemn, a man with whom I should quarrel more
than anyone if we were not united by affection, has for years
lived in rooms opening on to a flat roof by the sea."[21] What they

---

[19] *The Variorum Edition of the Plays of W. B. Yeats*, ed. Russell Alspach

(New York, 1969) 569.

[20] Yeats, *Letters*, 746.

[21] Yeats, "A Packet for Ezra Pound," in *A Vision*, 1-2.

talked about was poetry, as before, but also about religion and politics, and on each subject they had a few points in common but many points of contrast. Yeats tactfully advised Pound to steer clear of politics: "Do not be elected to the Senate of your country. I think myself, after six years, well out of that of mine. Neither you, nor I, nor any other of our excitable profession, can match those old lawyers, old bankers, old business men, who, because all habit and memory, have begun to govern the world." Unfortunately, Pound did not follow Yeats's advice to stay away from politics; if he had, he might have avoided much of the controversy of his later years. As for religion, Yeats and Pound were unorthodox believers, but believers nevertheless, as Yeats went on to say:

> I have been wondering if I shall go to church and seek the company of the English in the villas. At Oxford I went constantly to All Souls' Chapel, though never at service time, and parts of *A Vision* were thought out there. In Dublin I went to Saint Patrick's and sat there, but it was far off, and once I remember saying to a friend as we came out of Sant' Ambrogio in Milan, "That is my tradition and I will let no priest rob me."

In the end, Yeats made up his mind to avoid worship services at Rapallo: "I shall haunt empty churches and be satisfied with Ezra Pound's society and that of his traveling Americans." Pound, for his part, was as much opposed to organized religion as Yeats, though in his *Guide to Kulchur* in 1938 he recalled saying to Yeats: "Anticlericalism is no good (it being known between us fairly well what we did and did not believe). I can see a time when . . . we will have to join the Monsignori against Babbitt."[22] And Yeats had replied, "But CONfound it! In my country the church IS Babbitt." Pound, like Yeats, took the tolerant view of Christianity of a liberal Protestant, allowing him to borrow freely from its tradition without any obligation to subscribe to its doctrines. "I cd. be quite a 'good catholic,'" Pound wrote, "if they wd. let me pick my own saints and

---

[22] Pound, *Guide to Kulchur* (New York: New Directions, 1938) 155.

theologians."[23] From the viewpoint of his later, more orthodox Anglo-Catholicism, Eliot placed both Yeats and Pound among the modern heretics in *After Strange Gods: A Primer of Modern Heresy* (1933), and it was certainly a reasonable view of their unorthodox beliefs—although to be fair to them, it should be said that they both presented notable images of Christ in their poetry, Pound in his early "The Ballad of the Goodly Fere" and Yeats in his later "Two Songs from a Play," while Eliot never presented Christ directly in his poetry, even in his later period.

But poetry absorbed most of their attention at Rapallo in 1928 and 1929, and Yeats wrote with open admiration of Pound's collected shorter poems, the *Personae* of 1925, and more critically of the *Cantos*, which Pound was just bringing to the number of thirty, about a third of the whole sequence. Of the *Personae* Yeats wrote:

> One is a harder judge of a friend's work than of a stranger's because one knows his powers so well that his faults seem perversity, or we do not know his powers and think he should go our way and not his, and then all in a moment we see his work as a whole and judge as with the eyes of a stranger. In this book just published in America are all his poems except those Twenty-seven Cantos which keep me procrastinating, and though I had read it all in the little books I had never understood until now that the translations from Chinese, from Latin, from Provencal, are as much a part of his original work, as much chosen as to theme, as much characterized as to style, as the vituperation, the railing, which I had hated but which now seem a necessary balance. He is not trying to create new forms because he believes, like so many of his contemporaries, that old forms are dead, so much as a new style, a new man.

Yeats frankly admitted that he could not yet understand the *Cantos*, though he knew there was much fine poetry in them:

---

[23] Pound, *Guide to Kulchur*, 189.

I have often found there brightly printed kings, queens, knaves, but have never discovered why all the suits could not be dealt out in some quite different order. Now at last he explains that it will, when the hundredth canto is finished, display a structure like that of a Bach Fugue. There will be no plot, no chronicle of events, no logic of discourse, but two themes, the Descent into Hades from Homer, a Metamorphosis from Ovid, and, mixed with these, mediaeval or modern historical characters. He has tried to produce that picture ... where everything rounds or thrusts itself without edges, without contours—conventions of the intellect—from a splash of tints and shades: to achieve a work as characteristic of the art of our time as the paintings of Cezanne ... as *Ulysses* and its dream association of words and images, a poem in which there is nothing that can be taken out and reasoned over, nothing that is not a part of the poem itself.

So, in *A Packet for Ezra Pound*, Yeats gave his fullest view of Pound's work, and though Pound reacted irritably to it in a letter, saying that "if Yeats knew a fugue from a frog, he might have transmitted what I told him in some way that would have helped rather than obfuscated his readers,"[24] it remains a generally helpful and favorable opinion of Pound's achievement up to that time. To it, Yeats added only a few words in his introduction to *The Oxford Book of Modern Verse*, which he edited in 1935, saying that he found "more style than form" in Pound's poetry, but that Pound had "more deliberate nobility and the means to convey it than any contemporary poet known to me."

Pound was less fair to Yeats in those years, as we know from the account Yeats gave in his preface to *The King of the Great Clock Tower*, the play he published in 1934, where he recounted the humiliating experience of going "a considerable journey to get the advice of a poet not of my school who would, as he did some years ago, say what he thought." After inviting Pound to dinner at Rapallo, Yeats said he told Pound, "I am in

---

[24] Pound, *Letters*, 293.

my sixty-ninth year" and "probably I should stop writing verse,
I want your opinion of some verse I have written lately."
According to Yeats, Pound did not even ask him to read it
aloud, as would have been their custom in earlier years, but took
the manuscript away without comment, and "next day his
judgment came and that in a single word 'Putrid.'" Certainly
Pound's rudeness was uncalled for, and Yeats could only take
consolation in the relative success of the play. It strained the
friendship between the two poets, and they did not meet again,
except briefly in London in 1938, when Pound was on his way
to the United States in a futile attempt to try to keep his native
country out of the impending Second World War—a war in
which Pound would ill-advisedly take the side of the Italian
Fascists, leading to his imprisonment in the U.S. Army Detention Camp at Pisa and eventually in Saint Elizabeths hospital in
Washington. It is the dark side of Pound's career, his six months
at Pisa and thirteen years in St. Elizabeths, and yet he made
literary capital of it, for he published *The Pisan Cantos* and
wrote the later Cantos there, which, despite their controversial
nature, contain many brilliant poetic passages that are an
essential part of his whole achievement. Among the best of
them are his reminiscences of the friendship with Yeats during
the London years, some forty years earlier, and their encounters
in Rapallo in the later years:

> "Sligo in heaven" murmured Uncle William
>> when the mist finally settled down on Tigullio
>>> *Canto LXXVII*

The friendship between the two men lasted in the younger poet's
mind long after the older poet's death in 1939, and Pound did
try to make amends after the fact for the breach he had caused.
The last word in the poetics of their friendship was spoken by
Pound, when he placed Yeats among the secular saints of his
poetic Paradise, along with Ford and Joyce:

> Lordly men are to earth o'ergiven
>> these the companions:
> Fordie that wrote of giants
>> and William who dreamed of nobility
>>> and Jim the comedian singing:

> "Blarrney Castle me darlin'
> you're nothing now but a StOWne"
> *Canto LXXIV*

It was poetry that drew them together, and it is their poetry that remains as the chief record of their friendship and of their high achievement as writers. During the twenty years of their closest friendship, from 1909 to 1929, they learned from each other, criticized each other, borrowed from each other, and shaped each other's poetic style, fashioning, each in his way, a kind of Achilles' shield for confronting and reflecting their age, a destructive period in Western history, where the poet himself, whether Yeats or Pound, is a tragic actor in the midst of catastrophic changes, struggling for a unifying personal vision in a time of cultural disintegration. Yeats's apocalyptic vision of his time was expressed in many different ways, nowhere more strikingly than in the early "Valley of the Black Pig":

> The dews drop slowly and dreams gather: unknown spears
> Suddenly hurtle before my dream-awakened eyes,
> And then the clash of fallen horsemen and the cries
> Of unknown perishing armies beat about my ears.

Near the end of his life, Pound reached far back in his memory for a final echo from Yeats, when he wrote, in the notes for one of the last Cantos:

> That I lost my center fighting the world.
> The dreams clash and are shattered—
> And that I tried to make a paradiso terrestre.

The poetics of their friendship is preserved in the terrestrial paradises of their poetry, and however different they may sound, some echo of their singing together will always be heard.

6

POUND AND ELIOT: EDITING *THE WASTE LAND*

"The thing now runs from 'April...' to 'shantih' without a break."
So Pound wrote to Eliot when he returned the manuscript of
The Waste Land, after advising Eliot to cut the poem to about
half its original length. Though it was still Eliot's work, Pound
had helped him distill what he had written into a Super-Imagist
poem, concentrating its imagery, varying its rhythm, unifying
its theme, and making it the central masterpiece of twentieth
century poetry. The resulting poem shocked readers by its
originality, but in fact it came at the end of the first decade of
Modernism, the culmination of a revolutionary period of
experiment with poetic form and language that had been led by
Pound and crystallized by Eliot. In January, 1922, when he
finished editing the manuscript, Pound called it "the justification of the 'movement,' of our modern experiment, since
1900."[1]

　　According to Eliot, it was a "sprawling, chaotic poem"
he laid before Pound in Paris in late 1921. Pound helped him
shape it into the poem he published, which, Eliot later said, "left
his hands, reduced to about half its size, in the form in which it
appears in print."[2] That happened nearly a century ago; the
poem still challenges readers. Today *The Waste Land* stands at
the center of Modernism, a work of inspired collaboration
between two master poets. We can now look at the facsimile of
the edited manuscript, which itself adds a further set of Notes to
The Waste Land, and compare what Eliot originally wrote with
what Pound encouraged him to leave out. To do so is to gain
some insight into the way these two poets worked with poetic
language. Principally, it tells us that Pound's concern was with
precision of language and variety of rhythm, with what might be
called the *aesthetics* of the poem, putting into practice on a

---

[1] Pound, *Letters*, 180.

[2] T. S. Eliot, "Ezra Pound (1946)," 28.

longer poem his earlier Imagist prescription for shorter poems, while Eliot was primarily concerned with theme, with what might be called the *ethics* of the poem, drawing on his earlier philosophical studies to portray the decadence of Western civilization, suffering as he saw it from increasing materialism and diminishing spirituality. Eliot's chosen subject was the modern city in general and London in particular, and he voiced his devastating critique of it impersonally, chiefly through ironic contrasts of past and present. Pound's contribution was to eliminate most of the didacticism and discursiveness. The effect was to condense and unify the poem, to make the expression more powerful by reducing the number of words, paring the poem down to its essential meaning, excluding any passage that smacked more of imitation than parody, letting the dense texture of ironic allusions have their full impact. Pound did not try to make it *his* poem; he made it more definitely *Eliot*'s poem, preserving the conversational tone and informal, often slangy dialogue, but giving greater force to the imagery and greater variety to the rhythm than were evident in the original manuscript.

Pound gave Eliot credit for writing the greatest modern poem. Eliot gave Pound credit for helping him say what he wanted to say. The edited drafts, the result of their collaboration, he sent to their lawyer friend and patron, John Quinn, in New York, to thank him for his generous financial support, and to say that "In the manuscript of *The Waste Land* I am sending you, you will see the evidences of his work, and I think that this manuscript is worth preserving in its present form solely for the reason that it is the only evidence of the difference which his criticism has made to this poem...."[3] Quinn willingly accepted Eliot's gift, but since he died suddenly in 1924, just two years after the poem was published, his papers became the property of his wife, then of their daughter, who sold it to the New York Public Library in 1958, where unfortunately it became lost until after Eliot's death in 1965. Since Pound was still alive, Valerie, Eliot's widow, enlisted him as her primary consultant when the manuscript was discovered and shown to

---

[3] *T. S. Eliot, The Waste Land, A Facsimile and Transcript of the Original Drafts, Including the Annotations of Ezra Pound*, ed. Valerie Eliot, (New York: Harcourt Brace Jovanovich, 1971) xxiv.

her in 1968. She edited and published the facsimile in 1971, adding her own Introduction and Notes. Eliot had died thinking it was lost; Pound spoke for them both when he wrote her that "'The mystery of the missing manuscript' is now solved." The mystery was indeed solved, and it was finally evident just how much the most celebrated poem of the century owed to Pound's editing. John Quinn wasn't as sure as Eliot was of Pound's editorial work, saying when he wrote to thank him for the manuscript, "Personally I should not have cut out some of the parts that Pound advised you to cut out," but most readers have agreed that what Pound took out improved the finished poem. Few critics have seriously suggested restoring the lines Pound deleted; most have found his editorial work to be just what Eliot thought it was, "irrefutable evidence of Pound's critical genius." Eliot would eventually pay his debt in full, by dedicating the poem "To Ezra Pound, *il miglior fabbro*," "the better crafts-man," which had been Dante's tribute to Arnault Daniel, the Provençal troubadour from whose art he had learned, whose shade he had imagined as it dived into the refining fire of the *Purgatorio*.

Eliot's poem was the last fruit of a working friendship that started when they met in London in September of 1914. Pound was then serving as foreign correspondent for Harriet Monroe's new *Poetry* magazine in Chicago, and was searching for new talent to grace its pages. When Eliot showed him the manuscript of "The Love-Song of J. Alfred Prufrock," Pound immediately wrote an enthusiastic letter to Harriet Monroe from London on September 30 to say:

> I was jolly well right about Eliot. He has sent in the best poem I have yet seen or had from an American. PRAY GOD IT BE NOT A SINGLE AND UNIQUE SUCCESS. He has taken it back to get it ready for the press and you shall have it in a few days.
>
> He is the only American I know of who has actually trained himself and modernized himself *on his own.* The rest of the *promising young* have done one or the other but never both (most of the swine have done neither). It is such a comfort to meet a man and not have to tell him

to wash his face, wipe his feet, and remember the
date (1914) on the calendar.[4]

Eliot promptly returned the manuscript of "The Love-Song of J.
Alfred Prufrock" to him in early October, no doubt elated that
Pound had become his champion, for he had written it years
earlier and tried unsuccessfully to get it published, despite the
aid of his Harvard classmate Conrad Aiken. Pound sent the
finished text to Harriet Monroe with a brief note: "Here is the
Eliot poem. The most interesting contribution I've had from an
American. P.S. Hope you'll get it *in* soon." Miss Monroe was
not as prompt in publishing it as Pound had been in supplying
it, for in spite of his initial urging and subsequent badgering,
she had some misgivings about the poem which delayed
publication until the following June, though Pound never ceased
urging it on her. He found her objections so exasperating that he
wrote her on November 9, a month after sending her the poem:
"No, most emphatically I will not ask Eliot to write down to any
audience whatsoever. I dare say my instinct was sound enough
when I volunteered to quit the magazine quietly about a year
ago. Neither will I send you Eliot's address in order that he may
be insulted."[5] The following January, three months after sending her the poem, he gave her a further piece of his mind:

> Now as to Eliot: "Mr. Prufrock" does not "go off
> at the end." It is a portrait of failure, or of a
> character which fails, and it would be false art to
> make it end on a note of triumph. I dislike the
> paragraph about Hamlet, but it is an early and
> cherished bit and T.E. won't give it up, and as it
> is the only portion of the poem that most readers
> will like at first reading, I don't see that it will do
> much harm
>
> For the rest: a portrait satire on futility
> can't end by turning that quintessence of futility,
> Mr. P. into a reformed character breathing out
> fire and ozone.[6]

---

4 Pound, *Letters*, 40.

5 Pound, *Letters*, 44-45.

6 Pound, *Letters*, 50.

It is easy to understand why Eliot trusted Pound with editing his later and longer poem, since he had clearly shown how well he understood this first shorter poem. Pound had to go on needling Harriet Monroe to get it published, ending a letter to her on April 10: "*Do* get on with that Eliot," until she finally relented, and brought the poem out in June of 1915. The importance of this historical event was not lost on Pound, who told her it was the best poem *Poetry* had printed that year, and plumped for the annual prize to be given to Eliot, but plumped in vain.

As Valerie Eliot recognized, it had been "at Pound's insistence" that "Prufrock" was finally published, and she gave Pound credit for knowing Eliot better than his family did. "Shrewdly realizing that his future as a writer lay in England," she says in her Introduction to the Facsimile, "Pound encouraged him to settle there and to marry an Englishwoman, Vivienne Haigh-Wood." Pound did even more: in an extraordinary gesture of friendship, he agreed to write a letter to Eliot's father, Henry Ware Eliot, who did not approve of either the English residence or the English wife. In June, 1915, the month Eliot married, and the month his first important poem was published, Pound wrote Eliot's disapproving father back in St. Louis that his son was suited to be a poet, not a philosopher, and that he should settle down in England rather than America, with an English wife. Pound cited, to support his opinion about Eliot's true calling, his own successful career as an American expatriate poet in London, who had in a few short years, from 1908 to 1915, "engineered a new school of verse now known in England, France, and America," (he meant Imagism) and who regarded T. S. Eliot as his most promising discovery, and pledged Eliot's father "I shall continue to use such influence, as I have, in his behalf to get his work recognized."[7] Pound's letter did not have the desired effect; it did not convince Eliot's father to become reconciled with his son, but it proved conclusively to Eliot that Pound was a friend and fellow-artist who would do anything in his power to help him.

And so, just a year after they met, their friendship was sealed for good. It had to weather many strong disagreements afterward. Though both were American expatriates, they had followed quite different paths on their way to London. Pound

---

[7] Eliot, *Letters*, 103.

was born in a mining town on the Idaho frontier and schooled in Philadelphia and New York, and went first to Venice before moving to London, while Eliot was born in a large Missouri city and schooled in Boston, and was on his way to Oxford, on a traveling fellowship from Harvard to complete his doctorate in philosophy, when he met Pound in London. Their family background was just as different as their birth and education. Pound's grandfather had been a successful politician in Wisconsin and a Congressman in Washington, while Eliot's grandfather had been a Unitarian minister and the founder of what became Washington University in St. Louis. Given their widely different backgrounds, it is surprising how quickly they became friends, but Eliot's poetry was the bond between them. Meeting Pound changed Eliot more than meeting Eliot changed Pound. Until then, Eliot had been committed to a career as a philosophy professor, but once he met Pound he abandoned the safer prospect of American academic life for the riskier prospect of literary life in England, despite his family's objections. Pound was perfectly sure it was the right choice for Eliot, and went to work for him at once, putting some of Eliot's short poems in his *Catholic Anthology* in 1915 and publishing Eliot's first book, *Prufrock and Other Observations*, in 1917. Eliot returned the favor, writing a long essay on *Ezra Pound, His Metric and Poetry* (published anonymously to avoid suspicion of collaboration) in New York in 1917. The two men shared poems with each other, and mutually influenced each other when they switched from writing free verse to writing the rhymed quatrains of Eliot's Sweeney poems and Pound's *Hugh Selwyn Mauberley*, which were based, according to Pound, on the French poems of Théophile Gautier, *Émaux et Camées*, and the early New England *Bay State Hymn Book*.

So Eliot was continuing their collaboration when he entrusted Pound with editing *The Waste Land*, though by 1921 Pound had moved from London to Paris and they were no longer in frequent touch with each other. It was a strategic move for Pound, who soon inspired a younger generation of American expatriate writers in Paris, Hemingway among them, but Eliot, now well established in London literary circles, worried about Pound's shrinking reputation in England, and voiced his concern to John Quinn in 1919: "The fact is that there is now no organ of any importance in which he can express himself, and he is becoming forgotten." He never doubted, however, that Pound was the right man to help him synthesize the long poem he had started writing in 1919 and presented to Pound in 1921.

Pound was ready for the task; he set aside his own work with characteristic generosity and edited Eliot's poem, to their mutual satisfaction. Most of his judgments about it were impeccable, with only one possible exception. He questioned whether Eliot should use as his epigraph a passage from Joseph Conrad's story, "Heart of Darkness" (ending with "The horror! The horror!") because "I doubt if Conrad is weighty enough to stand the citation." But he didn't insist, asking later "who am I to grudge him his laurel crown?" Eliot changed his epigraph anyway, picking a much more obscure quotation in Latin and Greek from Petronius' *Satyricon.* The Conrad quotation would have been apt, if Eliot had chosen to stick with it, but it was too recent, and was in English, whereas the Petronius quotation was in two Classical languages, and it brought in the Sibyl of Cumae, a link to Mme. Sosostris, the gypsy fortune-teller in the first section of the poem, as well as expressing (in Greek) what all the inhabitants of *The Waste Land* felt: the wish to die.

Pound's initial doubt about the epigraph was of little consequence, compared to his slashing out many lines in Eliot's manuscript and leading Eliot to strike out even more. In the end, Eliot's poem was still long, but much shorter than when he left the manuscript with Pound. From the original 700 plus lines, Pound excised—or caused Eliot to excise—more than 300, leaving 434 lines to be published. Eliot had second thoughts about so much compression, but Pound said firmly, "That is 19 pages, and let us say the longest poem in the English language. Don't try to bust all records by prolonging it three pages further." [8] In addition to the long poem, Eliot had given him six short poems: "The Death of Saint Narcissus," "Song for the Opherion," (later published by Wyndham Lewis) "Exequy," "The Death of the Duchess," "Elegy" and "Dirge." Pound read and commented on them, but advised Eliot not to publish them with the poem; Eliot followed Pound's advice and published the poem all by itself.

To appreciate Pound's editing, all a reader has to do is to read the opening lines Eliot presented to him. They were a long dramatic monologue in colloquial English about a riotous party, 55 lines of loose blank verse, starting:

---

[8] Pound, *Letters,* 169.

First we had a couple of feelers down at Tom's place,
There was old Tom, boiled to the eyes, blind,
(Don't you remember that time after a dance,
And old Tom took us behind, brought out a bottle of fizz,
With old Jane, Tom's wife; and we got Joe to sing
"I'm proud of all the Irish blood that's in me,
"There's not a man can say a word agin me").
Then we had dinner in good form, and a couple of Bengal
lights.
When we got into the show, up in Row A,
I tried to put my foot in the drum, and didn't the girl squeal,
She never did take to me, a nice guy—but rough;
The next thing we were out in the street, Oh was it cold!

Now think of the first lines of the poem as we know them. They were already in the manuscript, but were obscured by Eliot's lengthy prologue, which he then cut out, choosing to open instead with a description of London as a city more dead than alive, in the springtime when nature should be blossoming and human life should be joyous.

> April is the cruelest month, breeding
> Lilacs out of the dead land, mixing
> Memory and desire, stirring
> Dull roots with spring rain.
> Winter kept us warm, covering
> Earth in forgetful snow, feeding
> A little life with dried tubers.

This desolate image of the city evoked the Waste Land of the Grail legend, his new title. He had first called the poem "He Do the Police in Different Voices," a humorous phrase he borrowed from *Our Mutual Friend*, Charles Dickens's novel about London, which would have suited the original opening lines. But Eliot wisely crossed it out in favor of *The Waste Land*, a phrase taken from Jessie L. Weston's *From Ritual to Romance*, a work of cultural anthropology not published until 1920, just before the poem was written, based on Sir James Frazer's pioneering study of the roots of Western religion and culture, *The Golden Bough*, published in 1890. *The Waste Land* was a much better title to suit the new opening, which described

London as a city that was already dead spiritually and that showed few signs of physical life. The poem now started with a grim image of what Eliot elsewhere called "the living death of modern material civilization." He went on to develop his theme by means of sudden, dramatic shifts of scene and character, a far cry from the low drama of his first beginning lines. It was at Pound's suggestion that he changed "Terrible City" to "Unreal City," adding a visionary touch to the new title, and establishing a bitterly ironic tone from the beginning that lasted through the remaining sections of the poem.

Pound offered a few alterations of diction and rhyme in the second section to make the meter less "penty," as he indicated in the margin, less "tum-pum at a stretch," while retaining the air of faded elegance that suited the setting of a rich woman's boudoir. Eliot changed his title for this section from "In the Cage" (the title of a recent Henry James novel) to "A Game of Chess" (alluding to two seventeenth century plays by Thomas Middleton, one called *A Game of Chess* and the other *Women Beware Women*, the latter containing a scene in which a young wife is seduced while her mother-in-law plays chess) and opened it with lines now familiar but slightly changed from the original:

> The Chair she sat in, like a burnished throne
> Glowed on the marble, where the *swinging* glass
> Held up by standards wrought with *golden* vines
> From which *one tender* Cupidon peeped out

which became:

> The Chair she sat in, like a burnished throne,
> Glowed on the marble, where the glass [no longer "swinging"]
> Held up by standards wrought with *fruited* vines
> From which a *golden* Cupidon peeped out

These changes were minimal, but they enhanced the imagery, and a little further on, the nightingale's song was transformed by Pound's excisions from the wordy

> Jug Jug, into the dirty ear of death
> And other tales, from the old stumps and bloody
> ends of time

to the more succinct

> 'Jug Jug' to dirty ears.
> And other withered stumps of time.

Interestingly, Pound made almost no changes in the final scene of the second section, no doubt recognizing that the dialogue between two women in a pub was a much more skilful dramatic scene than the opening lines of the previous section, with more effective colloquial dialogue. Pound did make a couple of significant interpolations, prompting Eliot to change "a closed carriage" to "a closed car," a more modern form of transportation, and replacing Eliot's original "When Lil's husband was coming back out of the Transport Corps," a reference to the end of the First World War, with the racier slang of "When Lil's husband got demobbed."

Pound cut Eliot's lines more drastically in the third section of the poem, "The Fire Sermon." He penciled out forty beginning lines about a vaguely drawn female character named "Fresca" in order to let the third section start with another grim description of London, this time as seen along the dreary banks of the Thames:

> The river's tent is broken and the last fingers of leaf
> Clutch and sink into the wet bank. The wind
> Crosses the brown land, unheard. The nymphs have departed.

From these three lines, Eliot would later take out only the "and," leaving the rest intact. Pound's deletion of the Fresca passage brought Eliot's memorable opening description of London back into place, and prompted Eliot to eliminate another thirty lines about Fresca, who now no longer fitted this poem—though he used the name in "Gerontion," where Fresca is one of the lost souls who are "whirled / beyond the circuit of the shuddering Bear." Pound's comment on the Fresca passages was severe: he said that Eliot should stop trying to imitate the heroic couplets of Pope's "Rape of the Lock," because "Pope has done this so well that you cannot do it better, and if you mean this as a burlesque, you had better suppress it, for you cannot parody Pope unless you can write better verse than Pope—and you can't." [9] So Eliot chucked out Fresca altogether, and abruptly shifted his scene to the typist's flat, where "the young man carbuncular" seduces the compliant typist, while the Greek prophet Tiresias regretfully looks on. Eliot had originally written the seduction scene in rhyming quatrains, but he was led by Pound's comments to compress them into a shorter passage of mainly pentameter lines with occasional rhymes, thus adding more metrical variety to the poem. Pound made two telling changes in the diction of the "Mr. Eugenides" section: he induced Eliot to take out the hesitant "perhaps" before "a weekend at the Metropole" with the sarcastic comment "dam per'apsy," and he suggested that "abominable French" (that is, "bad French," a damning phrase) be improved to read "demotic French" (that is, "vernacular French," a more impersonal phrase) thus putting a *mot juste* in place of a didactic adjective.

It was the fourth section, "Death by Water," that sustained the most thorough cutting in the whole manuscript, since Eliot's original ninety lines, describing Gloucester fishermen he had once seen off the New England coast, was collapsed into just ten lines about an ancient Phoenician sailor, memorably pictured as drowning off the English coast. Pound had already taken out so much that Eliot asked him, somewhat plaintively, if he should scrap the entire section, "Perhaps better omit Phlebas also?" But Pound's response was emphatic: "I DO advise keeping Phlebas. In fact I more'n advise. Phlebas is an integral part of the poem; the card pack introduces him, the drowned phoen. sailor. And he is needed ABSOLOOTLY where he is. Must stay in." [10] Pound's response to Eliot's query demonstrates how well he grasped the poem as a whole: he saw that one fairly short part of it belonged, while many much longer parts did not. When Eliot asked Pound whether he should use "Gerontion" as a prelude to THE WASTE LAND, Pound replied just as emphatically, "I do *not* advise printing *Gerontion* as a preface. One don't miss it at all as the thing now stands. To be more explicit still, I advise you NOT to print *Gerontion* as a prelude." [11]

---

[9] Eliot, *The Waste Land, A Facsimile*, 127.

[10] Pound, *Letters*, 171.

[11] Eliot, *The Waste Land, A Facsimile*, 127.

In the fifth and final section, "What the Thunder Said," Pound made few suggestions, leaving it much as Eliot had written it, which implies that it was the most finished part of the poem and may have been written last. Pound did however suggest one significant change, and it was surprising that Pound should have been the one to suggest it to Eliot. Eliot had written "After the frosty silence in the garden*s*" to describe what is implicitly a crucifixion scene; Pound struck out the final "s," making it "After the frosty silence in the garden," subtly linking it to the Garden of Gethsemane where Christ prayed before his death. Thus Pound deftly increased the Christian allusions in the poem, which, for a long time after it was published, was regarded as anti-Christian, because it equated pagan religions such as Buddhism and Hinduism with Christianity, but which now is more often read in the light of Eliot's post-*Waste Land* conversion to Anglo-Catholicism, as a link to his later explicitly Christian poetry. This slight change was not a contradiction of Pound's earlier deletion of an explicit Christian reference from "The Burial of the Dead"—"I John saw these things, and heard them"—because there he removed a too obvious Christian allusion from a subtly ironic poem.

With Pound's invaluable editorial advice, and a little help from his wife, Vivienne, who doctored two conversational lines in the pub scene, Eliot published the poem in October, 1922, in the first issue of his new journal, *The Criterion*, in London, and in November, 1922, in *The Dial* in New York. In December, it was published in book form by Boni & Liveright in New York, with a few typographical corrections, and with Eliot's notes added for the first time, though he had been collecting them as he wrote the poem. Eliot was 34 years old and his reputation was made; Pound was 37 and his friendship had been proved. While writing it, Eliot was recovering from what was called a "nervous breakdown" (Eliot said it was not "nerves" or "insanity" but "psychological troubles"—fits of depression he had suffered before), and had gone first to Margate, near London, mentioned in the poem, then to a sanitarium at Lausanne (on Lake Geneva, called Lac Leman in the poem). He had given the manuscript to Pound in Paris as he returned from Switzerland in December, 1921. Pound condensed it and sent it back to Eliot, writing John Quinn that "It is about enough, Eliot's poem, to make the rest of us shut up shop."[12] It seems that Pound's praise did more to cure Eliot's depression than the Swiss psychiatrist could do, because Eliot wrote John Quinn jubilantly, before the poem was published, "I think it is the best I have ever done, and Pound thinks so too."[13]

At the risk of simplifying a highly complex poem, we can say that with Pound's help, Eliot had made the poem a SuperImage of The Modern City as The Waste Land. He had compressed his theme into a series of episodes and images, which implied allusively and ironically the theme that material improvement led to spiritual decay. Pound, as the chief architect of Modernism, knew how to guide Eliot in condensing his long poem, for his model was the brief Imagist poem, not a narrative but at its best a moment of revelation crystallized around an image. Eliot made it into a technique for effectively criticizing modern civilization by means of sharp contrasts of past and present, nature and city, the real city of London with the legendary Waste Land. By Pound's compression, the modern city had *become* the Waste Land, obsessed with matter and devoid of spirit. Eliot's poem revealed the dreariness of living purely on the physical plane, without belief in immortality, the inhabitants reduced to dead souls in living bodies. The five disparate sections of the poem formed a unified image of the city which is realistic, even naturalistic, but at the same time imagist and symbolist. The underlying myth, drawn from medieval romances, carried the implicit meaning that what was missing was a vision of the Holy Grail in the midst of the Waste Land, while Eliot's words carried the explicit meaning that there was a desperate thirst for spiritual life in the midst of physical death. The contrasting images of dryness and wetness give continuity to the poem, and there is symmetry in its beginning with "The Burial of the Dead," a ritual phrase from the Book of Common Prayer, now only "fear in a handful of dust," and ending with a Sanskrit prayer, "What the Thunder Said," the disembodied voice of God over the image of Christ Crucified ("the agony in stony places") and Resurrected ("who is that on the other side of you?"). Pound's strategic editing had helped Eliot make the imagery of city life into a more original and

---

[12] Eliot, *The Waste Land, A Fascimile*, xxii.

[13] Eliot, *The Waste Land, A Facsimile,* xxii.

shocking variety of rhythmical shapes than it was when he first wrote it.

Characteristically, Pound closed his collaboration with Eliot by attaching a satirical poem to the edited manuscript, a joking treatment of what they had done together, but Eliot wanted the world to see how much Pound had helped him, and in 1925, he added the now famous dedication "To Ezra Pound, *il miglior fabbro.*" The full meaning of this phrase was not clear until the facsimile of the manuscript was published in 1971. Then there was convincing evidence that Pound had indeed served as the

Sage Homme ("Male Midwife")

These are the poems of Eliot
By the Uranian Muse begot;
A Man their Mother was,
A Muse their Sire.

How did the printed Infancies result
From Nuptials thus doubly difficult?

If you must needs enquire
Know diligent Reader
That on each Occasion
Ezra performed the Caesarean Operation.

Cauls and grave clothes he brings,
Fortune's outrageous stings,
About which odour clings,
      Of putrefaction,
Bleichstein's dank rotting clothes
Affect the dainty nose,
He speaks of common woes
      Deploring action.

He writes of A.B.C.s
And flaxseed poultices,
Observing fate's hard decrees
      Sans satisfaction;
Breeding of animals,
Humans and cannibals,

> But above all else of smells
> Without attraction
>
> Vates cum fistula ["Seer with an Abscess" or "Prophet with a Boil"][14]

Pound added: "It is after all a grrrreat litttttttterary period." It was. The poem Eliot wrote and Pound edited was the final proof.

---

[14] Pound's letter to Eliot, first dated Dec. 24, 1921, but actually written Jan. 24, 1922, is in *The Letters of Ezra Pound, 1907-1941*, 170.

7

POUND'S POETIC PROGRESS: FROM IMAGE TO IDEOGRAM

The twentieth century was noted for its violence; it should be equally noted for its poetry. The century was indeed destructive, but it was immensely creative as well, and its creative achievement is what will be remembered longest. That achievement was not because of, but in spite of, the age, for as Pound said in *Hugh Selwyn Mauberley* in 1920,

> The "age demanded" chiefly a mould in plaster,
> Made with no loss of time,
> A prose kinema, not, not assuredly, alabaster,
> Or the "sculpture" of rhyme."

And so, if great poetry was written in the twentieth century, it had to be written in defiance of what the age demanded. And indeed, defiance was a keynote of modernism, for most modern poets were opposed to what passed for "modernism," in so far as it meant replacing men with machines in the rapid technological change which some called progress. Modern poets sought change, but of a different sort: a change in the way words were used. They were individualists, first and foremost, and many had an American way of using English, but above all, they were looking for new possibilities of expression because the old ways had grown stale. They quickly saw how the French Symbolists had made *vers libre* an alternative to meter, and they experimented with the English language until they had made it into a new vehicle for poetry.

Ezra Pound was at the center of this literary revolution, since he was the poet most responsible for the radical transformation of English poetic style which occurred in the twentieth century. T. S. Eliot, one of the revolutionaries himself, acknowledged that Pound was there before him, at the start of the

Imagist movement in London,[1] and R. P. Blackmur, one of the most perceptive critics of modern poetry, held that "Poets like Pound are the executive artists for their generation."[2] What Pound did was fundamental, even more fundamental than writing his own poetry: he showed other poets how to "Make it New," how to write poetry that seemed unprecedented, even though it derived from earlier poetry that Pound knew as much about as any man of his age. To make poetry new, he took models from languages other than English, or from poets who, if they wrote in English, lived before Shakespeare and the Elizabethans, poets in the Old English tradition of "The Seafarer" or in the Middle English tradition of Chaucer. It was Pound who led the way towards a new poetic style, successfully combining the ancient with the modern, the national with the international, the Eastern with the Western, so successfully that genuinely new poems could be written in English, a language that at the turn of the twentieth century had seemed nearly exhausted. Pound always maintained "It is tremendously important that great poetry be written; it makes no jot of difference who writes it."[3] The ambition was impersonal; the achievement was personal.

Pound was the one who actively promoted a new Renaissance, and fortunately, there were a number of gifted men and women who participated in it, with the result that the twentieth century became the greatest age for poetry in English since the Elizabethans. Such a statement may sound sweeping, but consider that the Elizabethans expressed a new English identity in their poetry by creating a new medium of expression for it, namely, blank verse, the iambic pentameter line, the standard poetic line in English from the early seventeenth until the early twentieth century. Pound and his contemporaries did something just as monumental when they replaced blank verse with free verse, and it was Ezra Pound, more than any other poet of the

---

[1] "The *point de repère* usually and conveniently taken, as the starting-point of modern poetry, is the group denominated 'imagists' in London about 1910. I was not there." T. S. Eliot, *To Criticize the Critic*, 58.

[2] R. P. Blackmur, "An Adjunct to the Muses' Diadem," in *Form and Value in Modern Poetry* (New York: Doubleday Anchor Books, 1957) 119.

[3] Ezra Pound, "A Retrospect," 10.

century, who deliberately set out to make free verse the dominant poetic form, in order to express as well as to defy the destructive age in which he lived.

That much is literary history now. But at first, even Pound did not know what the new poetic style would be. For almost a decade, Pound dabbled in the Late Romantic style which was then in vogue, with its flowery language, elaborate figures of speech, and regular meter and rhyme, mostly translating poems from other languages or imitating poems in the style of Browning or Swinburne or the earlier Yeats. He eventually came to dismiss all the poems published in his first book, *A Lume Spento*, which he brought out at his own expense in Venice in 1908 and carried with him to London, as "stale creampuffs," since they showed no obvious departure from contemporary English poetic practice at the turn of the century. Two of his early poems, "The Ballad of the Goodly Fere" and "Ballad for Gloom" ("God Our God is a Gallant Foe") were actually chosen for an anthology of Victorian poetry. They did not seem out of place there, even though the portrait of Christ in "The Goodly Fere" was hardly Victorian, since he was no "pale Galilean," à la Swinburne, but a more athletic and masculine figure, "a man o' men was our goodly fere." Pound's portrait of Christ was both realistic and Biblical; however, he used the old ballad form and a sort of modified Scots dialect for it, making the poem seem less a departure from the norm than it really was.

It was not until his seventh volume of poems, *Ripostes*, came out in 1912, that Pound clearly broke with traditional definitions of poetry and began to create a new poetic style, for which he invented the name Imagist. It was definitely a new movement in English poetry, even if Pound chose to pay homage to the French school of the *Symbolistes* by giving the name a French spelling and by calling his first anthology in 1914 *Des Imagistes*, his translation into French of what would have been *Some Imagists* in English. Imagism, however, was less French than Anglo-American, coming from a group of young poets who wanted to redefine poetry, and who, in 1909 in London, included the Englishmen T. E. Hulme, F. S. Flint and Richard Aldington, and the Americans Pound and H. D. Pound went on to declare H. D. the first Imagist, and the initials stuck with her, though Hilda Doolittle said she was unprepared, when she showed him a group of her poems in the British Museum tea room in 1912, for Pound to edit them right there in front of her, and then to send them off to be published in *Poetry* magazine in 1913, signed "H. D. Imagiste."[4] Their publication made Imagism a movement, but Pound soon stopped claiming a French origin for the Imagists, and induced another of them, F. S. Flint, to do a "History of Imagism" for *The Egoist* magazine in 1915 that made the movement definitely English. Pound (as we now know) dictated most of this founding document to Flint, and so he was in charge of its history, just as he was in charge of the three "rules" of Imagism published earlier in *Poetry* magazine. These rules called for poets to treat subjects directly, in as few words as possible, and with a musical rather than a metrical cadence, and to bear in mind the definition he provided: "An 'Image' is that which presents an intellectual and emotional complex in an instant of time."

The decade from 1910 to 1920 was the Imagist Decade, since a new movement emerged in English poetry with Pound as its leader, and a new poetic style was produced whose touchstone was the short lyric poem, a brief verbal image, without end rhymes and in the looser rhythm of free verse. Pound's revolution changed the way a poem looked and sounded: meter and rhyme were no longer requisites; poetry was defined by its imagery, its accuracy of language, and its musical rhythm. To exemplify the new mode, Pound himself wrote a number of Imagist poems, most of them in the three years from 1912 to 1915. The best known of these is "In a Station of the Metro," which has become so familiar that many readers of poetry can quote it from memory:

> The apparition of these faces in the crowd;
> Petals on a wet, black bough.

Here was a poem that fitted perfectly Pound's definition of the Image; it was "an intellectual and emotional complex in an instant of time." It was also a poem which owed much to the Orient, for Pound, explaining how he had written it after getting off a Paris subway one night, said he had started with a much longer poem, but condensed it to two lines to make it more like the short Japanese poem called the *haiku*, or as he said more "*hokku*-like." Pound not only created a new movement in English poetry with Imagism, but chose to model one of his own Imagist poems on a

---

[4] H. D., *End to Torment: A Memoir of Ezra Pound* (New York: New Directions, 1979) 18.

Japanese form, synthesizing at a stroke the Eastern and Western traditions into a new English poetic style. His model, he said, was a Japanese *haiku* which he translated as:

> The fallen blossom flies back to its branch:
> A butterfly.

Thus Pound's Metro poem, a touchstone of the new Imagist movement, made use of an Oriental model, a short poem wholly outside the Western tradition, in a non-Western language. Pound insisted the poem was nevertheless modern, because its setting was a crowded Paris subway station, a new urban subject for a poem. He took a normally dark and forbidding place, an ugly man-made setting, and transformed it into something surprisingly beautiful, by using a simple flower metaphor.

Pound wrote his "Metro" poem in 1912. In 1913 he deepened his knowledge of the East by starting to learn Chinese, a lifelong project from which he never wavered. He did so because, quite unexpectedly, he had received the manuscripts of an American scholar named Ernest Fenollosa, whose widow entrusted them to Pound in London because she said he was the only person capable of making sense of them. Pound made so much sense of them that he began to see Imagist poems in the Chinese language. To Pound, Imagism was reinforced by written Chinese characters; he believed images were implicit in Ideograms. As early as 1914, even before *Cathay*, he put into *Des Imagistes* translations from the Chinese, such as "Fan-Piece, for Her Imperial Lord," which was another example of the new English poetic style he called Imagism:

> O fan of white silk, clear as frost on a grass-blade,
> You also are laid aside.

It is clear that Pound had come to think that to be Oriental might be another way to be Modern.

Pound learned from the Chinese about poetry, as we know from Ernest Fenollosa's essay on "The Chinese Written Character as a Medium for Poetry," which Pound published with approving footnotes. He took Fenollosa's word for it that Chinese ideograms were "based upon a vivid shorthand picture of the operations of nature," and he accepted as literally true Fenollosa's explanations of Chinese characters, that "the ideograph meaning 'to speak' is a mouth with two words and a flame coming out of it." Pound accepted Fenollosa's teaching that Chinese was closer than English to *things*, that it was more concrete by its very nature because it was pictographic, made up of visual images rather than phonetic transcriptions of sounds. Fenollosa argued that "Poetry differs from prose in the concrete colors of its diction," a doctrine Pound readily accepted, since T. E. Hulme had earlier taught him that "Prose is a museum where all the old weapons of poetry [are] kept." In one of Pound's most revealing footnotes to Fenollosa's essay, he says that "The poet, in dealing with his own time, must also see to it that language does not petrify on his hands. He must prepare for new advances along the lines of true metaphor, that is interpretative metaphor, or image, as diametrically opposed to untrue, or ornamental, metaphor."[5]

What Fenollosa liked about Chinese was that "Its etymology is constantly visible." But Fenollosa was a foreign scholar of the Chinese language, not a native of China, and he had to acknowledge that "the pictorial clue of many Chinese ideographs can not now be traced," that is to say, the metaphorical nature of the ideogram is not always apparent to the Chinese who use the language. It was nonetheless Fenollosa's theory that "The prehistoric poets who created language discovered the whole harmonious framework of nature, they sang out her processes in their hymns." Pound followed Fenollosa's theory, for he believed that poetry could recover the "whole harmonious framework of nature" in a Western language like English, if it constructed verbal rather than visual ideograms, through words rooted in the concrete images from which, theoretically, all language originated.

So what Pound came to call the "ideogramic method" was not original with him, but came second hand from Fenollosa; however, it became original when Pound put it to practical use, in the complex verses of *The Cantos*. While writing these longer poems, he explained what he was doing in the prose of his *Guide to Kulchur* in 1938: "the ideogramic method consists of presenting one facet and then another until at some point one gets . . .

---

[5] Ernest Fenollosa, "The Chinese Written Character as a Medium for Poetry," edited by Ezra Pound (San Francisco: City Lights Books, copyright 1936, but first published in 1920) 23.

a just revelation irrespective of newness or oldness."[6] Pound was moving in composition from the short Imagist poem to the longer Ideogramic poem, but there was continuity in his progress, since he regarded both images and ideograms as separate poetic units, independent of other images or ideograms, and his mature style in *The Cantos* is a consecutive series of images combined into ideograms, which are capable of standing alone, or of being connected with other images or ideograms by free association, without benefit of logic.

If we look, for example, at *Canto LXXXI* , the best known of *The Pisan Cantos*, and to many readers the culmination of Pound's poetic work, we see that it can be resolved into a series of images which together form a verbal picture of Pound himself in the "gorilla cage" at Pisa, under arrest for treason against his native country, remembering earlier experiences but fully aware that at the moment he was inside a cage. It could be called "Self-Portrait at Pisa." The Canto begins by creating an image out of Greek mythology, "Zeus lies in Ceres' bosom," an image of the Marriage of Heaven and Earth, doubles it with an image from Confucius, "Taishan [the sacred mountain of China] is attended of loves," and then proceeds to recall Pound's long-ago visits to Spain, "in 1906 and in 1917," when he saw a series of Velazquez paintings in the Prado museum in Madrid. His mind becomes filled with a procession of images of human culture, ranging from primitive folk dances to the American Revolution, placed beside images of the American prison camp where the guards are sometimes benevolent toward their prisoner, "thank Benin for this table ex packing box, 'doan yu tell no one I made it,'" and also beside a personal anecdote of the philosopher-poet George Santayana as a young Spanish boy arriving in Boston with his lisping speech, and then of Pound's own father in a folksy conversation with an American journalist about an American senator. Suddenly Pound interposes his own invented lyric about English music, with its memorable refrain, "Lawes and Jenkyns guard thy rest / Dolmetsch ever be thy guest"—his tribute to English culture at its finest, since Lawes and Jenkyns were earlier English composers, and Dolmetsch was a contemporary maker of ancient musical instruments whom Pound knew in London—all

---

[6] Pound, *Guide to Kulchur* (New York, New Directions, n.d.—originally published in 1938) 51.

this in a poetic composition which itself may be taken as another form of English culture. He then remembers Chaucer's lines, "Your eyen two wol sleye me sodenly / I may the beauté of hem not susteyne," harking back to an earlier English poetic culture, followed by "for 180 years almost nothing," that is, no great poetry between Chaucer and Shakespeare in the English tradition. Then he has what seems to be a personal vision, "there came a new subtlety of eyes into my tent," and he concludes the Canto with the finest of all his lyrics, beginning "What thou lovest well remains." These moving lines are an ideogram in themselves of Pound's tragic situation, a visionary poet with dreams in his head, placed in a prison surrounded by guards, transcending his circumstances through the quality of his vision: "First came the seen, then thus the palpable / Elysium, though it were in the halls of hell," he asserts, as he gives a compelling glimpse of an invisible Heaven in the midst of a visible Hell. He denounces his own earlier arrogance, "Pull down thy vanity," with its Biblical echo, which Hugh Kenner in a review of Pound's correspondence with his wife Dorothy traced to his reading of the book of Ecclesiastes in the prison camp at Pisa,[7] and asserts that nature is a greater artist than man, "The ant's a centaur in his dragon world," and not even a fashionable Paris designer of *haute couture* like Paquin can improve on natural beauty: "The green casque has outdone your elegance." Finally, Pound in condemning his overweening pride nevertheless argues that he has done something worthwhile with his life, for "To have gathered from the air a live tradition / or from a fine old eye the unconquered flame / This is not vanity." Ecclesiastes, or the Preacher, had lamented that "All is vanity" and that "there is nothing new under the sun," but Pound insists that despite the vanity something new was created, that new work came out of old models, and that what has been called his "creative mistranslation" of Chinese resulted in the transformation of English into a new language for great poetry.

All in all, Pound's *Canto LXXXI* can be seen to form an ideogram or mosaic of his state of mind in 1945 in the prison camp at Pisa, a poet of marvelous powers and accomplishments who has through his own impetuosity and stubborn willfulness, in

---

[7] Hugh Kenner, "What Prison Taught the Poet," review of *Ezra and Dorothy Pound: Letters in Captivity, 1945-46,* in *The Wall Street Journal* (Friday, Feb. 5, 1999): W10.

short, his vanity, subjected himself to punishment and humiliation. His rootedness in Greek mythology and the English poetic tradition is clear, as well as his fondness for music and painting, sister arts, and his newly discovered appreciation for little acts of kindness by his fellow men. Nowhere in the vast extent of his poetry does Pound give a more appealing self-portrait: *Canto LXXXI* is the summing up of his entire career. It is an ideogram of Pound at Pisa in its full complexity: the old poet still in possession of his artistic gift but reduced, through no one's fault but his own, to the most humiliating public shame.

It helps us understand what is going on in *Canto LXXXI* if we read it as an Ideogram of Pound himself at Pisa, and it also helps us overcome their admitted difficulty if we call all *The Cantos* Ideograms. Their difficulty is intrinsic; so far, the sequence has not yielded to any general explanation, however ingenious, of its often baffling obscurities. But, if we think of *Canto LXXXI* as an Ideogram, a longer poem made up of smaller poems converging into a larger image, it begins to have the spatial coherence of a mosaic. The figure of Pound in the prison camp at Pisa is the picture of a highly civilized mind suffering extreme physical degradation. An Ideogram is more spatial than temporal, as Chinese characters are spatial in comparison with phonetic languages like English, though poetry is still a temporal art, dependent on the sounds of words and the rhythm of breathing. But to think of a poem as Ideogram is like thinking of it as Imagism, more akin to pictorial art than to narrative art. *Canto LXXXI* portrays the many different facets of Pound's personality, his childhood memories of Spain, the voice of his father, the Greek myth of the god Zeus embracing the goddess Ceres as if it were Heaven on Earth, which he likens to the Chinese image of the sacred mountain, Taishan, surrounded by worshippers, one of the guards making a table from a packing-box in the gorilla cage at Pisa, a letter from Adams to Jefferson after the American Revolution, a letter from H. L. Mencken to Pound about economics, the playing of handmade ancient musical instruments in London by a man Pound knew and admired, a ghostly apparition entering his tent, and finally and most movingly, Pound's enduring legacy of poetry made from what he loved best, even in the shameful situation where he found himself, grasping "the palpable Elysium though it were in the halls of hell." *Canto LXXXI* is an ideogram of Pound himself in the prison camp at Pisa; it is a late self-portrait in words. It has lasted half a century and is likely to last much longer. We may not be able to explain it fully, but we can never get it out of our minds, once we have read it.

That is just a sample, but it is a crucial sample, of Pound's evolution from Image to Ideogram, a movement central to the century of Modernism in which he lived. His experiments helped to start a new poetic tradition. We have much great poetry in English as a result of his work and that of his fellow poets, Yeats and Frost, Eliot, Stevens, and Ransom, to name some of the best. John Crowe Ransom was head of the rival school of Southern Fugitives, who criticized the Imagists and resisted the early influence of Pound, but as editor of the influential *Kenyon Review* in the middle of the century, he wrote an essay about "New Poets and Old Muses," where he conceded that Pound's way of remaking the tradition had been necessary and fruitful:

> The new poet today looks back upon a half-century which may have been more eventful for new poetry than any other in the history of our language, with the exception of the second half of the 16th century, and possibly its successor the first half of the 17th century. . . . Mr. Ezra Pound advised the poets early to "Make It New," and there was never a better time for this advice than the impoverished period from which they had to start. They founded many innovations, and engineered many revolutions. Before long an *avant-garde* was galloping off in almost every direction and it was difficult in the confusion to tell which one the main troops were going to follow. That was a magnificent confusion. All possible poetries were being tried, and nothing could have been better for the times.[8]

Without Pound's introduction of Eastern as well as Western poetic models into English, and his urging other poets to try similar experiments with language, it is unlikely that the Modernist revolution would have been so successful. Yet, as

---

[8] John Crowe Ransom, "New Poets and Old Muses" (1948) reprinted in *Selected Essays of John Crowe Ransom*, ed. Thomas D. Young and John Hindle (Baton Rouge: Louisiana State University Press, 1984) 319.

Ransom said, it produced great poetry, drastically altering the earlier English poetic tradition that had been dominant since the late sixteenth century. "To break the pentameter, that was the first heave," Pound wrote in *Canto LXXXI*, a recognition that new poetry resulted from going outside the tradition, from making a deliberate break with Shakespeare. Yet Pound was right in claiming "This is not vanity," for Shakespeare was not forgotten; he was simply no longer the chief model of poetic invention. He had been imitated creatively by poets as great as Keats, but Pound's "mutation" was an abrupt departure from the Elizabethan tradition, and it allowed a new style of English poetry to be born. By the middle of the twentieth century, there was a new tradition in English poetry, and for the first time since the late sixteenth century, a non-Shakespearean poetry prevailed. Pound led the way from the Image to the Ideogram, neither of which depended on Shakespeare, nor indeed, on exclusively Western models. Pound showed that genuinely new English poems could be written without regular meter and rhyme, and he introduced new models for poets to follow: the Image became the new model for short poems, the Ideogram the new model for long poems. Pound wanted to write both short and long poems, but didn't want to continue writing sonnets (though he could do so if he chose, as demonstrated by "A Virginal") and he didn't want to write tragedies, comedies, or epics (though he thought of *The Cantos* as "that great forty-year epic"). What he set out to do was to write poetry in English for a modern audience, and the Image and the Ideogram were his means of creating new poems that did not depend on traditional English poetic forms. Images were brief verbal pictures in free verse; Ideograms were complex verbal structures in free verse. They were his dual means for the creation of new English poems clearly different from any English poems of the past. As e. e. cummings, one of the most innovative poets of the century, said later of Pound, he was "the authentic 'innovator,' the true trailblazer of an epoch,"[9] which was his way of acknowledging the breakthrough Pound had made, and paying Pound tribute as the chief architect of Modern poetry in English.

Pound's Imagism was part theory and part practice; his Ideogram was less theory than analogy, or metaphor, which he

---

[9] *Selected Letters of e. e. cummings*, edited by F. W. Dupee and George Stade (New York: Harcourt, Brace & World, 1969) 254.

put into practice. Like Yeats's gyres, which he said in *A Vision* were to be understood as "metaphors for poetry" rather than actual geometric figures, Pound's ideograms were diagrams for longer poems, based on Chinese characters as interpreted by Ernest Fenollosa, an American Orientalist Pound never met. Pound's ideograms apply especially to *The Cantos*, but just as Imagism includes poems like Eliot's "Preludes," which were never part of the Imagist movement, so the "Ideogramic Method" Pound extracted from Chinese can be stretched to cover such notable longer poems as *The Waste Land* or *Paterson* or *The Bridge*, poems which may be called SuperImagist, which have no plot or narrative continuity, but are detailed constructions of a larger visual pattern. Without a picture in mind that is largely supplied by its title, *The Waste Land* would be even more unfathomable, and the same is true of *Paterson*, which depends on an image of the New Jersey city where William Carlos Williams lived, while *The Bridge* is a series of poetic perspectives by Hart Crane on the actual metal structure of the Brooklyn Bridge. The Ideogram may be called a SuperImage, though Pound preferred to take his analogy from the Chinese language, to think of his longer poem as a mosaic of images like Chinese pictograms, concrete radicals combined into a complex whole. It takes nothing away from Pound's analogy to say that the Chinese do not see in their characters what Pound saw in them. His theory of the Ideogram is validated by his poems, and the poems are valid enough in themselves, however difficult to grasp. Oriental readers, schooled in the associative images of the Chinese Ideogram, may have less trouble understanding Pound's poetry than Western readers who are accustomed to narrative continuity.

At any rate, Oriental models like the Japanese *haiku* and the Chinese ideogram helped Pound instigate the remarkable revolution in English poetic style which we now call Modernism. His poetic progress was from the short simple image like the *haiku* to the longer complex poetry of *The Cantos*, which he understood to be analogous to the Chinese written character. There were many other influences on his poetry, of course, from Classical Greek lyrics to Latin elegies to Anglo-Saxon meters to French Symbolist *vers libre*. But the influence of the East on Pound was crucial to his development as a poet, even if we grant that he made the Orient what he wanted it to be rather than taking it as it was. Pound's Imagist poems could never be mistaken for Japanese *haikus*, nor could *The Cantos* be mistaken for Chinese calligraphy, but he saw in these Eastern languages something his Western languages could not give him, and they helped him produce a change in English poetry that influenced other poets as well. As he said in one of his footnotes to Fenollosa, "the poet, in dealing with his own time . . . must prepare for new advances along the lines of true metaphor." Given Pound's inventive genius, ancient Oriental models, along with contemporary French and Classical Greek models, helped him "make it new" in his own language, and helped him make the twentieth century a great period of English poetry.

8

POUND'S POETIC SELF-PORTRAITS

In 1914, in an article on "Vorticism," which he wrote for the *Fortnightly Review*, Pound made an explanatory statement about himself which is often quoted:

> "In the 'search for oneself,' in the search for 'sincere self-expression,' one gropes, one finds some seeming verity. One says 'I am' this, that, or the other, and with the words scarcely uttered one ceases to be that thing.
>
> I began this search for the real in a book called *Personae*, casting off, as it were, complete masks of the self in each poem. I continued in long series of translations, which were but more elaborate masks."[1]

By the time he wrote that much about himself, Pound had published several books of poems, and he knew that many readers were baffled by his frequent changes of personality and mood, ranging all the way from his early hero, Bertran de Born, the French troubadour in "Sestina: Altaforte" who glories in fighting battles, to the later figure of the delicate Chinese girl in "The River-Merchant's Wife: A Letter" who waits in patient, lonely vigil for her husband to return from a long journey. Though these two figures are totally unlike each other, and are even different sexes, both were masks for Pound, who had learned much more from Browning than how to write *Dramatis Personae*. Browning had taught him that a lyric poet could speak through characters quite different from himself, and the practice became so familiar to Pound that in time he became more prolific than Browning at masking himself. Certainly Browning wrote a number of memorable character sketches,

---

[1] Pound, "Vorticism," First published in *The Fortnightly Review* XCVI (N.S.) (September 1, 1914); republished in *Gaudier-Brzeska* (New York: New Directions, 1960) 85.

speaking with the voices of Renaissance Italian painters such as "Andrea del Sarto" and "Fra Lippo Lippi," or of religious figures such as the English prelate in "Bishop's Bloughram's Apology" and the Jewish prelate in "Rabbi Ben Ezra," but Pound went farther afield, bringing to life as his own *personae* the real but nearly forgotten medieval troubadour Bertran de Born in "Sestina: Altaforte" and "Near Perigord," and the mythical Ulysses of Homer's *Odyssey* in several poems, especially in his first *Canto*.

Pound was producing more than just characterizations, real or fictional: he was engaging in something akin to reincarnation, a possibility he had raised in one of his earliest poems, "Histrion" (its title appropriately drawn from the Greek word for a theatrical mask), which is worth looking more than once:

> No man hath dared to write this thing as yet,
> And yet I know, how that the souls of all men great
> At times pass through us,
> And we are melted into them, and are not
> Save as reflexions of their souls.
> Thus am I Dante for a space and am
> One François Villon, ballad-lord and thief
> Or am such holy ones I may not write,
> Lest blasphemy be writ against my name;
> This for an instant and the flame is gone.
>
> 'Tis as in midmost us there glows a sphere
> Translucent, molten gold, that is the "I"
> And into this some form projects itself:
> Christus, or John, or eke the Florentine;
> And as the clear space is not if a form's
> Imposed thereon,
> So cease we from all being for the time,
> And these, the Masters of the Soul, live on.

John Berryman argued in *The Freedom of the Poet* that the subject of all Pound's *Cantos* was Pound himself.[2] It is a

----

[2] See Berryman's essay on "The Poetry of Ezra Pound" (1949) in *The Freedom of the Poet* (New York: Farrar, Straus & Giroux, 1976) 253-69.

perfectly valid opinion, as long as we recognize that "Pound himself" means many other selves. Like his hero and alter ego Ulysses, Pound was "many-minded," a highly complex personality incorporating multiple individuals. All Pound's shorter poems are justly called *Personae*, because they are all himself, a self that could become almost anything it wanted to become— even, in his earliest important poem, "The Tree":

> I stood still and was a tree amid the wood,
> Knowing the truth of things unseen before;
> Of Daphne and the laurel bow
> And that god-feasting couple old
> That grew elm-oak amid the wold.
> 'Twas not until the gods had been
> Kindly entreated, and been brought within
> Unto the hearth of their heart's home
> That they might do this wonder thing;
> Nathless I have been a tree amid the wold
> And many a new thing understood
> That was rank folly to my head before.

If Pound could transform himself into a tree, he could become anything, and his very versatility is part of what makes him difficult, for it makes every reader wonder, who is the real Ezra Pound? By his own admission, he wore many different masks during his career; we are bound to ask which one is the most authentic. It is here that his longer poetic self-portraits hold a special fascination, because, like the painted self-portraits of Rembrandt or Van Gogh, they seem to be portraits of the same artist at different moments of his life, as a younger and an older man.

Think not only of such remarkable translations as "The Seafarer" or "Homage to Sextus Propertius," both of which have elements of self-portraiture in them, but of his two most explicit self-portraits: *Hugh Selwyn Mauberley: Life and Contacts* and the *Pisan Cantos*. *Mauberley* was published in 1920, when Pound was 35, when his Imagist phase was ending and he was leaving London for good, to go first to Paris and eventually on to Rapallo. *Pisan Cantos* was published in 1948, when he was over 60, and when, because of his notorious Rome radio broadcasts during the Second World War, he had been imprisoned as a traitor in an American military camp at Pisa.

These two major self-portraits employ quite different techniques, equally fragmentary but equally convincing. In
Mauberley, he used a variation of the Imagist technique he had
invented, presenting a series of short poems focused on an
imaginary poet much like himself in London. In the *Pisan
Cantos*, he used the later technique he adapted from the Chinese
Ideogram, forming a mosaic of fragmentary images into a complex image of Pound as a prisoner at Pisa. His later portrait is
not fictional: it is Pound himself in the most desperate situation
of his life. If we place these two familiar but quite different
portraits side by side, we can see images of the poet at two
widely separate moments of his life and career. In the first, the
Mauberley sequence, he is bidding a poetic farewell to London,
after successfully starting Modernism by initiating a new
literary style in English. The poem, however, begins with a
mock-epitaph, and throughout the work he treats himself
satirically, as if he were a dilettante, a failed aesthete, who is
aware that the First World War has just ended, but who regards
it as largely a waste of talent:

> There died a myriad,
> And of the best, among them,
> For an old bitch gone in the teeth,
> For a botched civilization.

In the second, the *Pisan Cantos*, he has become the tragic
victim of his own self-destructive behavior at the end of the
Second World War, which he views as another human catas-
trophe—the sequence opens with "The enormous tragedy of the
dream in the peasant's bent shoulders"—but which cannot
prevent him from describing himself in chaotic yet brilliant
poetry. Comparing them, it seems as if Pound first masks and
then unmasks himself in his two extended poetic self-portraits.

The analogy with the famous self-portraits of Rembrandt
and Van Gogh is relevant, because in the paintings we see
depths in each man's face, reflecting the unfathomable character
of the artist behind them. We have no doubt that the artist is
seeing himself truly, even though he may be Rembrandt
wearing a ridiculous hat or Van Gogh with a bandage on his ear.
The likeness of the artist in Pound's *Hugh Selwyn Mauberley* is
less close to life than these visual self-portraits, because the
artist behind it is wearing the mask of his fictional character.

The likeness in the *Pisan Cantos* is however closer to the paintings, because the artist portrays himself realistically, seemingly without a mask, though at times he appears remarkably detached from himself, more an observer than a victim. Pound's self-portraits of the younger and older artist present, first, a youthful and ironic likeness, and later, an aging and tragic likeness.

Even closer analogies to Mauberley than the youthful self-portraits of Rembrandt or Van Gogh are the two autobiographical characters who were well known to Pound when he wrote his poem: Stephen Dedalus and J. Alfred Prufrock. *Hugh Selwyn Mauberley* could also be called *A Portrait of the Artist as a Young Man*, as Joyce's title indicates and as Eliot's poem implies. As a character, he is as original a creation as they are, a fictional poet with the highest ambitions, an American poet from "a half-savage country," which is the United States in an earlier century, but what part of it we aren't told, quite possibly from a Western frontier town like Hailey, Idaho, where Pound himself was born. Mauberley the American poet has come to London to seek his literary fortune, exactly as Ezra Pound did in 1908. But for all his apparently uncivilized origins, Mauberley is a sophisticated and serious artist, and so though he meets the right people—among them Mr. Nixon the literary critic and Lady Valentine the fashionable hostess—he is unable to find their world of social pretension and artistic self-promotion satisfying, and so he is forced to accept "his final / Exclusion from the world of letters," and to fade slowly out of sight, far from London, the literary capital of the English-speaking world, adrift somewhere in the South Pacific, like Paul Gaugin in Tahiti, perhaps, although lacking Gaugin's ability to transform the tropical scene into a landscape of the imagination. Poor Mauberley, who once dreamed of resuscitating "the lost art of poetry" and of maintaining "'the sublime' in the old sense," and who left behind at least one poem, his "Envoi," as proof of his true ability as an artist, resigns himself to what the London literary set wanted to think he was:

> "I was
> And I no more exist;
> Here drifted
> An hedonist."

And he goes on dreaming idly of beautiful women, like the golden-haired singer in "Medallion"—his last "Envoi" or formal farewell to London.

This brief summary of Pound's complicated poem is enough to place Mauberley where he belongs, beside Stephen Dedalus and J. Alfred Prufrock. He is, like each of them, the author's double, a thinly disguised self-portrait ironically presented, but, unlike Stephen Dedalus, he is a failure, a portrait of the artist as a young man without a future, and unlike J. Alfred Prufrock, he has actually accomplished something in his short literary career, even if being in London "three years, out of key with his time," has brought him little but scorn. Joyce's autobiographical hero, Stephen Dedalus, is so much like his author, who abruptly left his native Dublin to go to Paris and become a famous writer, that it is only at the very end of the novel the reader can see he isn't Joyce after all, but rather an amazingly self-confident young man, who has renounced the priesthood that was offered to him, the summit of a young Irishman's ambitions, for an uncertain career as a writer, a writer whose only literary work up to that point is a love-poem faintly reminiscent of Shelley, but not the equal of Shelley at his best. Mauberley, in contrast, has imitated Edmund Waller successfully in his "Envoi," leaving behind in London a poem true to its model, "Go, Lovely Rose." René Taupin, in studying how Pound converted French Symbolism into Anglo-American Imagism, remarks that "True influence consists in surpassing one's model, not in reproducing it,"[3] and Pound showed such mastery on behalf of his alter ego, Mauberley, who is the fictional author of a more complex, though not necessarily finer, poem than the song of Edmund Waller which it effectively echoes. Thus, Mauberley has proved he is a young artist capable of writing a genuinely new poem, something which Stephen Dedalus never conclusively proves. But surprisingly, at the end of Pound's poem, Mauberley accepts failure and goes into self-imposed exile far away from London, while at the end of Joyce's novel, Stephen is on his way from Dublin to Paris, full of high aspiration "to forge, in the smithy of my soul, the uncreated conscience of my race." Joyce's unfulfilled artist leaves Dublin sure of his promise, whereas Pound's successful

---

[3] Taupin, 171.

artist leaves London resigned to his defeat: the contrast between these two autobiographical figures couldn't be clearer.

Nor could it be clearer in the case of Mauberley and Prufrock. Prufrock is self-condemned, a "prude in a frock coat" as his name suggests, who sees himself as the object of ridicule, "with a bald spot in the middle of my hair." He would like to be a heroic figure: Lazarus miraculously come back from the dead, or John the Baptist martyred for his faith, or Prince Hamlet avenging his father's murder, but he knows he is far from being any of them. He hears mermaids singing in his dream, but says "I do not think that they will sing to me." Mauberley on the other hand *does* hear the sirens singing to him—and in Greek:

> Ἴδμεν γάρ τοι πάνθ', ὅσ' ἐνί Τροίη
> ["we know all you did in Troy"—
> from Line 189, Book 12, of Homer's *Odyssey*]

The ineffectual Prufrock reluctantly awakens from his dream of sirens singing to the sound of human voices mocking him. Prufrock is more neurotic, more fictional, less autobiographical than Mauberley. His dreams are all wish-fulfillments, and his failure is the fantasy of a man unable to act in life—he does not even, like Henry James's John Marcher, live by the illusion that he might capture an imaginary beast in the jungle of a London drawing room. Prufrock sees himself as a complete failure; Mauberley on the other hand accepts the failure that is thrust upon him. Mauberley is not Pound, as Pound once had to insist,[4] but he is more like Pound than Prufrock is like Eliot, and his failure does not come from some inner lack of talent, or inability to act decisively, but from the failure of others to find merit in his work. Prufrock is a mock-hero, a dreamer although a profound one, while Mauberley is a real artist whose fate was to produce the "'sculpture' of rhyme" in an age which demanded "an image of its accelerated grimace." Eliot's poem is about a man who fails to achieve his dreams, while Pound's poem is about a man whose age failed to live up to his dreams.

There is another major difference between these three equally arresting youthful portraits of the artist. Mauberley is

---

[4] "Of course, I'm no more Mauberley than Eliot is Prufrock." So Pound wrote in a letter to Felix Schelling, Pound, *Letters*, 180.

not only a fictional character but a deliberate mask for the author, while Stephen Dedalus and Prufrock are both fictional characters resembling their authors. We know Mauberley is a mask, because we can often see Pound holding it in front of him—starting with the suggestive subtitle, "E.P. Ode Pour L'Election de son Sepulchre" (an alteration of Ronsard's "Ode: De L'Élection de son Sepulchre") right through being "born in a half-savage country" (that is, America) to his "Audition of the phantasmal sea-surge" (Pound loved to quote Line 34, Book One, of Homer's *Iliad*, describing the sound of the surf rolling in to shore, παρά θῖνα πολυφλοίσβοιο θαλάσσης, "by the shore of the loud-roaring sea") all the way to imagining "his final / Exclusion from the world of letters." Pound's poem seems so much like his life that it has intrigued readers, ever since it was published, with the puzzle: who is Pound and who is Mauberley? We know the real Pound left London voluntarily for Paris and Rapallo. But we also know that Pound, though unpopular with some English writers whom he had scorned in print, was never totally excluded from "the world of letters" in London, since he was taken very seriously by the writers he respected: especially Ford, Yeats, Joyce, Eliot, H. D., and D. H. Lawrence, not to mention his fellow-Imagists, T. E. Hulme, F. S. Flint, and Richard Aldington. So, how could Pound possibly have thought himself a failure? Mauberley seems all too willing to give up the struggle; Pound never gave it up; in fact, Pound relished intellectual combat. Mauberley is not a brilliant but self-deluded dreamer like Prufrock, for he has proved himself a genuine artist like the real Pound; his fault is that he is too susceptible to the condemnation of others, the "non-esteem of self-styled, his 'betters,'" meaning the literary establishment of the day, who want to exclude him from "the world of letters." In the end, Mauberley renounces the London literary scene; he is not rejected by it. Pound thus has ingeniously used Mauberley as his ironic mask, as the disguise he needed to make his escape from London.

When we come, much later in Pound's career, to his self-portrait in the *Pisan Cantos*, we know that he has long ago left London behind, and has enjoyed the adulation of disciples in Paris and Rapallo, only to suffer the ignominy brought upon him by his well-meaning but clearly misguided Rome Radio broadcasts, followed by the physical torment of the open cage at Pisa. His older self-portrait, as a prisoner in the American military detention camp, is quite unlike the younger self-portrait, which was of an artist ironically detached from himself. It is more like those later self-portraits of Rembrandt and Van Gogh, realistic and profoundly tragic. Still more, it is like King Lear, Shakespeare's tragic hero, whose vanity blinded him to the difference between his good and evil daughters, and whose madness reduced him to being a "poor, bare, forked, animal," forced at last "to feel what wretches feel." Pound at Pisa was so reduced in circumstances from Mauberley in London that he was robbed of ironic detachment, unable to conceal himself behind a mask, and grateful for small acts of kindness from fellow prisoners, which he dutifully records:

> And Mr. Edwards superb green and brown
> > in ward No. 4 a jacent benignity,
> of the Baluba mask: "doan you tell no one
> > I made you that table"
> > > > *Canto LXXIV*

He has sunk so low he looks sympathetically at the tiny crawling creatures he can see from his cage:

> Brother Wasp is building a very neat house
> of four rooms, one shaped like a squat Indian bottle
> > La vespa...
> > > ....
> > an infant, green as new grass,
> > has stuck its head or tip
> > out of Madame La Vespa's bottle...
> > > ....
> > The infant has descended,
> > > from mud on the tent roof to Tellus
> like to like colour he goes amid grass-blades
> > greeting them that dwell under XTHONOS
> > > > *Canto LXXXIII*

There can be no doubt that "Old Ez," Pound at Pisa, is a much fuller self-portrait, more than a hundred pages longer than the portrait of the young Mauberley in London, but now, instead of the dashing figure of the young, ambitious poet who resigned himself to the role of failed aesthete, it is the haunting figure of an aging, condemned man, who sees himself most compellingly as the victim of his own vanity, "a beaten dog beneath the hail, / A swollen magpie in a fitful sun" (*Canto LXXXI*). Though the age still has its faults, as Pound notes bitingly from time to time, the man has greater faults than the age. If he once knew the heights of aspiration, he now knows the depths of despair, as he admits in the touching image that ends the whole sequence:

> If the hoar-frost grip thy tent
> Thou wilt give thanks when night is spent.
> *Canto LXXXIV*

What redeems him from self-pity, into which he otherwise would surely have sunk, is the power of his imagination and his unfailing gift for expression, which allow him to retain some degree of dignity in the most painful circumstances. The *Pisan Cantos* are Pound's portrait of the artist as an old man who has "been hard as youth sixty years," who imagines himself as "a lone ant on a broken ant-hill," but who can nevertheless rouse himself to heights of eloquence in the midst of humiliation. If, in *Hugh Selwyn Mauberley*, he had wanted "to maintain 'the sublime' in the old sense'," in the *Pisan Cantos*, he has maintained the sublime, despite his circumstances.

Strangely enough, Pound at Pisa is more American than was Mauberley in London. Despite his "half-savage" origins, Mauberley was eager to please Londoners and to become a part of the English literary world. The older Pound has shed his air of British refinement for an outspoken American frankness, with occasional dashes of dialect humor straight out of the Old West: "the pride of all our D.T.C. was pistol-packin' Burnes" he says, or he asks "'runnin whisky' sez he; mountain oysters?" or expressing, as he often does, what he calls "the virtue *hilaritas*," he reports a conversation he overhears:

> "Hey Snag wot are the books ov th' bibl'?"
> "name 'em, etc.
> "Latin? I studied Latin."
> said the nigger murderer to his cage-mate
> (cdn't be sure which of the two was speaking)
> "c'mon, small fry," sd/the smaller black lad
>   to the larger.
> "Just playin'"
> *Canto LXXVI*

Pound seems to take genuine pleasure in the Americans that are around him, both his guards and his fellow-prisoners, as if he were among compatriots, not among foreigners. There are 41 names of Americans in the *Pisan Cantos*, and they are not there by accident, for as he notes in another humorous passage, the names have national significance: "all the presidents / Washington Adams Monroe Polk Tyler / plus Carrol (of Carrolton)," such are the familiar names he hears around him in the DTC at Pisa, and a few lines later, he quotes approvingly the saying of Confucius that "filial, fraternal affection is the root of humaneness." In one of the most amusing passages, Pound dryly comments on the limitations of army slang, which he seems to delight in using freely, enriching the texture of his own high poetry:

> the army vocabulary contains almost 48 words
> one verb and participle one substantive ὕλη ("matter")
> one adjective and one phrase sexless that is
> used as a sort of pronoun
>
> *Canto LXXVII*

It seems curious but undeniable that Pound felt his American identity most strongly in the Pisan prison camp where he was trapped as an alleged traitor, and therein lies a tragic irony.

Rather than say that he has unmasked himself in this later self-portrait, it might be truer to say that he has exchanged the comic mask for the tragic mask. The earlier mask was satirical and in a broad sense comic. The later mask is clearly tragic, even with flashes of ironic humor, but it is, after all, a mask, because Pound is still behind it, still writing poetry as magnificently as ever. The difference between the younger and older poet is the difference between his comic and his tragic mask, and also between a fictional poet who writes a love song to a mysterious lady, "her that sang me once that song of Lawes," and a real poet who writes a song to all that he has loved, affirming that "What thou lovest well remains," that is, the whole range of things remain that he has loved in a life devoted to poetry and beauty. Indeed, at the center of the younger and older self-portraits are lyric passages of surpassing beauty: the "Envoi" in the middle of *Mauberley*, and "What thou lovest well remains" in the middle of the *Pisan Cantos*. It is worth noting that Pound in London, like Mauberley in his

"Envoi," was chiefly celebrating Beauty, an aesthetic ideal outlasting time, while Pound at Pisa was chiefly celebrating love, an emotion so powerful it drives him to affirm, in spite of his personal humiliation, that "What thou lov'st well shall not be reft from thee." If the tragic mask mirrors the degradation of the caged poet, the true poet can still sing of "Elysium, though it were in the halls of Hell." What we admire about Pound, both early and late, is his poetic gift, and it is never more evident than in the *Pisan Cantos*. So if the later self-portrait reveals "a man on whom the sun has gone down," it also reveals one who was able "to break the heave of the pentameter," to launch Modernism with the perfecting of free verse, and who "gathered from the air a live tradition, and from a fine old eye the unconquered flame." Pound the prisoner could sing in his prison, exhibiting a rare capacity for poetic invention which prompted H. D.'s stunned admiration: "It isn't sad. There is a reserve of dynamic or demonic power from which we all may draw. He lay on the floor of the Iron Cage and wrote the *Pisan Cantos*."[5]

And so Pound's moment of greatest humiliation proved to be his moment of greatest poetic power. His poetic self-portraits, in *Mauberley* and in the *Pisan Cantos*, different as they are, are alike in their poetic mastery, which never deserted him early or late, young or old. The comic mask suits the younger Pound as the tragic mask suits the older Pound; he is there behind them both, the poet whose changing personae reflect his multi-faceted personality, but also, and just as surely, his unfailing poetic gift. Mauberley and Old Ez are strongly contrasting but equally unforgettable self-portraits, two different faces of the same great, flawed poet.

---

[5] H. D., *End to Torment*, 44.

9

THE GREATEST POET IN CAPTIVITY: EZRA POUND AT ST. ELIZABETHS

I first visited Ezra Pound at St. Elizabeths Hospital in Washington, D.C., in the spring of 1955. The circumstances were a little odd, but just as clearly providential, since meeting Pound profoundly influenced my life and my career. I had been recalled to military service during the Korean war from graduate study at Vanderbilt University; recently married, I was living in an apartment in Falls Church, Virginia, from which I commuted daily to the Pentagon, where I was serving as a congressional liaison officer in the Office of the U.S. Navy Judge Advocate General. The visit to Pound was prompted by a chance acquaintance with a young psychiatrist, Dr. Michel Woodberry. He told me Pound welcomed visitors and, learning of my interest in Pound (I was engaged in research for a doctoral dissertation on Pound, Eliot, and Henry James), he encouraged me to write to Pound. Without this friendly word of advice, I never would have summoned up the courage to write and ask if I could come to see him. Soon I had a reply, scrawled on a sheet of typing paper in Pound's customary abbreviated style:

> Dear Mr. Pratt:
> By all means. Write to Superintendent S. Liz for permission. Thursdays are best. I like slow talk can't crowd into ¼ hr. Visiting hours 2-4 Sat. Sun. Tu. Th.
> E.Pound

So I wrote to Dr. Winfred Overholser, then superintendent of St. Elizabeths Hospital, who a decade earlier had testified at Pound's hearing on the charge of treason; he approved my visit simply because Pound was willing to see me. One afternoon early in May, I drove out from the Pentagon; I changed on the way from my navy uniform into civilian clothes, afraid I might make the wrong impression on a man accused of treason if I arrived in military dress.

I drove into the prisonlike compound of the hospital with some apprehension about Pound's mental state. Pound had been incarcerated for more than a decade, and I was unsure how accustomed he might be to seeing strangers; but I was put at ease as soon as I met him on the spacious grounds outside the drab interior of the hospital. It was a sunny spring day, and it was reassuring to find Pound seated under a tree in a reclining lawn chair, holding court with some bohemian young people, two women and two men. I was not prepared for his appearance, since I thought of him as a dashing figure with red hair and beard, and discovered instead an elderly and portly figure with a white tuft of beard who wore an old wool-lined hunting cap. I had read Eliot's account of Pound in his younger days in London, when he wore such bizarre costumes that only his socks were conventional enough to be worn by anyone else, and I noted with sadness that his style of dress had degenerated along with his physique: he was clad in a loose and faded sportshirt gaping at the navel, baggy trousers, unlaced shoes, and, alas, no socks. Without standing up, he reached his right hand over his left shoulder to greet me, and when I introduced myself, he introduced me in turn to his disciples, David Horton (of the Square Dollar series of economic, political, and philosophical pamphlets Pound was then publishing) and William McNaughton (another pamphleteer whose literary-cum-polemical leaflet was called simply "Strike"), an Asian-looking young lady who knew Chinese, and another very slim girl who told me she was from a Jewish family in Nashville and was distantly acquainted with my wife (a native of Nashville). This motley band of disciples hardly rivalled Pound's circle early in his career, but there was one dignified figure central to the group around Pound—the poet's wife, Dorothy Shakespear Pound, a handsome elderly woman who said very little but who spoke with a cultivated British accent and listened to everything. I found Dorothy more sympathetic immediately than Ezra, and I came to think of her affectionately as his true Penelope, although in time I began to feel more comfortable with him, too, even spending one rainy afternoon alone with him in one of the wards of the hospital.

My outdoor visits with Pound were relatively relaxed, and in the midst of earnest conversation with him—he did most of the talking, of course—I could almost forget the surroundings. But my indoor visits were depressing, because the other inmates were constantly walking about and talking to themselves, the odor of the hospital was offensive, and the drabness of the bare walls and floor almost made me feel I was a prisoner. Pound himself, however, hardly seemed aware of his surroundings: the clearest memory I have of him is of a man intent on his thoughts, able to concentrate even amid the constant distractions of a mental asylum. He stood for me then, and stands for me still, as a supreme example of the power of mind over matter, an impression more than confirmed by the productivity of those thirteen long years as a prisoner of the state, when he proved he was indeed the greatest poet in captivity by writing the later Cantos and translating classics ranging from the Chinese of Confucius to the Greek of Sophocles.

I was alone with Pound only that once in a half-dozen visits; most of the time I would be one of five or six people, who always included Dorothy Pound, and at other times included Craig LaDriere, a professor at Catholic University. (Pound joked with him about attending the Modem Language Association convention, or MLA, which Pound referred to in one of his characteristic puns as "the mêlée.") By June I felt enough at ease in Pound's company to ask if I could invite into the circle an old friend, James Dickey, then a young and promising poet just returning from a stay in Europe on a *Sewanee Review* fellowship, who was eager to meet Pound. Twice I brought my wife; she made a hit with Pound by presenting him with a freshly baked tin of cookies one Sunday afternoon. She also won his favor by her knowledge of French (she had done a master's thesis at Vanderbilt on the plays of Paul Claudel and the philosophy of Gabriel Marcel), and he enjoyed trying out one of his innumerable word games on her. He wrote out on a scrap of paper "Pas de leur on que nous" and asked her to read it aloud so that it came out as "Paddle your own canoe" to everyone's amusement. So the visits were generally sociable, and Pound was never happier than when surrounded by a group of people raptly listening to him talk. I found it hard to credit the stories I heard of him later, when he had returned to Italy and was reported to sit for hours without saying anything. The silent Pound I never knew; the Pound I knew was eager to talk with anyone who would listen.

I listened a great deal, and so did everyone who came to see him. Some of his talk was economic or political, since his obsessions with money and government that had persisted from the thirties were unflagging. On the first afternoon he produced an Italian newspaper headed *Il Secolo* 4 maggio 1955. I did not know Italian then, but I recognized his name and a few of the words beside it, "*economia...poèta...usuria.*" There was also a photograph of him, slouched in the same aluminum lawn chair he was seated in before me, and he talked excitedly of how his patent formula for peace and prosperity via Social Credit was being publicized in Italy, his adopted country. "It will open their eyes," he said, his own eyes shining as he spoke. "An end to all this mendacity: we will put the truth before the people. It's all a question of money. . . ." He pulled out a cheap plastic billfold from his pocket and held up a dollar bill for all of us to see. "Here," he said, "is American money—on the front is a portrait of George Washington, and on the back is a pyramid and a Coptic eye—you know the Masonic order had much to do with founding the republic." I had read that Washington and other founding fathers of the United States were Masons, but for the first time I noticed that there is a Masonic emblem on our currency. "Well," he went on, "that dollar is scarcely worth the paper it's printed on. Is that honesty? Is that the way to run a country? Money should be a cer-TIF-i-cate of value for work performed. If you read Douglas and Gesell, you'll see what I mean. The only time I got close to Muss', I gave him eighteen questions. He reduced them all to one simple declarative statement, which he put in his next big speech: ECONOMIC ORDER IS THE BASIS OF SOCIETY. He didn't have to be told twice."

Pound grew more and more animated, the white tuft on his chin shaking as he warmed to the subject: "People don't believe I was given freedom of speech in Italy! Yet they introduced every broadcast on Rome radio with: 'In keeping with the Fascist policy of granting free expression to those who are qualified to speak, Mr. Pound is given the right to voice his own opinions without restriction....'" These broadcasts over Rome Radio in the early forties were, we all knew, the principal cause of his being indicted for treason, yet he defended them as "exercises of free speech by a patriotic American."

When I later read the transcripts of those broadcasts at the Library of Congress, I could understand both why he was indicted and why he thought he was only practicing his right of free speech. The messages were a combination of personal opinions and poetry of the sort Pound had been delivering for years in print to a mainly literary audience; but delivered over an enemy radio station in wartime to an audience of American troops and their allies, his broadcasts were no longer acts of criticism but acts of betrayal. Pound consistently maintained that he spoke as an American with his country's best interests in mind. As I heard him declare his innocence, it was clear to me that he had never understood the limitations of free speech. If he had made the same broadcasts inside the United States, even in wartime, he might have been dismissed as a crank; but the United States had declared war on Italy, and from enemy territory, speaking against his country, he was bound to be branded a traitor. This was the only real evidence of insanity I saw in Pound: he seemed not to understand the charges against him. This opinion is confirmed by something Pound wrote about himself. In an unpublished letter now in the Humanities Research Center at the University of Texas, Pound wrote to Ronald Duncan on April 15, 1958, shortly before his release from St. Elizabeths: "You may say I was nuts to the extent that it never entered my poetic head that a charge of treason COULD be trumped up."

The psychiatrists testifying at Pound's indictment argued that he was incompetent to stand trial because he could not understand the charges, an argument that still seems reasonable to me. Those who have contended—always from a distance—that Pound was only being protected by the psychiatrists, who used the insanity defense solely to keep him from being tried, have always seemed to me to miss the point, because, for all his brilliance, it was obvious to anyone who talked to him that Pound was unable to recognize the simple difference between free speech and treasonable provocation, a line that he had unknowingly crossed. I came to believe that Pound was being sufficiently punished for his crime: thirteen years in a prison-hospital is a long sentence under any circumstances, and if he thought himself free to broadcast in Italy, he couldn't help knowing he was not free, for a long time afterward, as a result. He could have visitors, yes, but he could not leave the gates of St. Elizabeths as they did. I felt a little guilty about leaving him there, though I did not pity him, because he was able to surmount all circumstances and do what he could do best— namely, write. Some of the best of Pound's writing and translation came out of his imprisonment, and so no admirer of Pound can regret that punishment. Nor can any detractor hold that he went unpunished, whether or not the psychiatrists' plea of "mentally unfit to stand trial" was correct in 1945. In 1955 I thought he was not mentally fit to stand trial: even after ten years he still did not understand the charges against him.

In those hours of conversation he gave relatively few moments to obsessions with economics and politics. He talked mostly of other writers, his friends of the London years before and during World War I: Yeats and Ford and Eliot, Aldington and Hulme. From the first he treated me as a fellow writer, almost as a potential collaborator, just as he had once treated them, a treatment which I found both flattering and exhilarating. He assumed I was an equal; even knowing that I was not, I could appreciate at once how Pound must have struck other writers in those great years of literary invention when a new style was being collectively formed and Pound was at the center of it. Everyone who came to him, then or later, was welcomed into the writer's profession, and regarded as someone who had definite ideas about the craft, about how to "make it new" and to produce new literary works that might be masterpieces. Pound took the vocation of writing as the most important calling on earth, and he treated all other human beings as potential writers, no matter how modest their talents. All of Pound's writing, early and late, is addressed to other writers, trying to help them understand what literary greatness is; and his mind naturally went back to the writers he had learned most from himself, principally Yeats and Ford. He said: "I used to see Yeats on Mondays and Ford on Tuesdays, because the two couldn't stand each other, and I learned more from Ford than from Yeats, because Ford always talked sense, and Yeats sometimes talked sense and sometimes silliness." He also talked about older writers he admired, particularly Thomas Hardy. "Hardy always kept his attention on the subject, and let the style take care of itself. To him a robin was a robin, and a squirrel was a squirrel"—he pointed at some visible animals on the hospital grounds—"none of this cake-shop decoration writers are producing today." He turned and looked directly at me as he said this: "You could be thirty years ahead of your time if you followed Hardy: concentrate on the subject; that's what matters." I was a little taken aback at being compared to Thomas Hardy, but when I realized that Pound was speaking to me as a potential writer, I realized he too was talking sense.

When the others got up to go, that first afternoon, I started to leave with them, but Pound protested: "Mr. Pratt, you aren't leaving? I must talk with you some more. What is it you're studying?"

"The European tradition in American literature," I replied hesitantly.

"Ah," he said, brightening. "These fellows today are making poetry an adjunct of the arts—*Little Review* sort of stuff. They don't see the DIMENSION. Dimension is what you find in older poets. You take Bryant, for instance, or Whittier ... They weren't just poets. Everybody knows Bryant wrote 'Thanatopsis.' But few people know he once hit a man over the head with his cane for insulting Andy Jackson. They think of Bryant as an old man with a long beard, but they haven't got his dimension."

He was pursuing his favorite subject now, with Dorothy Pound and me as his only listeners, and I was avid to hear more.

"I mean to say, fifty years ago we had to find a way to write. English couldn't be used to convey what a man was thinking. So we experimented with technique. Now all you hear about is technique. If they'd quit trying to find out whether such-and-such a word, in such-and-such a Canto, came from whatever dead volume or dead language, and got down to the subject.... Hardy was right; he told me something that made sense. When everyone else in the twenties was talking of technique, he showed that the man who stuck to his subject was the man to watch. Sure, you've got to have style ... but the subject is what counts."

I asked him if he thought any older American writers had helped to shape the modern tradition, and he said yes, but that his generation had to avoid being influenced too much by their elders in America: that was why they left the country and went to Europe. "Take Henry James," he thundered: "James had to get away from the shadow of Hawthorne, so he went to France and learned from Flaubert. Take Eliot: he had to escape from too much Emerson, and so he went to England and learned from Henry James. Take Cummings: he had too much of Thoreau in him before he went to France. And take me: I had too much Longfellow, and I had to go abroad for Dante and the Troubadours." (I wished he would go on with the list—citing Williams, perhaps, as having too much Whitman, and Hemingway, who had too much Twain, and Faulkner, who had too much Poe—but unfortunately Pound stopped with himself.)

I later mentioned an article I had read by Richard Aldington, Pound's fellow Imagist, in which he had criticized Pound and Eliot as poets of "the library and the town," and praised D. H. Lawrence as a poet of "nature." Pound did not seem annoyed. "I haven't heard from Richard for a while," he said, "but I always say that one good attack is worth twenty eulogies." The Pound of *Ripostes* and *Instigations* came vividly to life with this remark, and I understood how as a young poet he had thrived on literary controversy—even though later it would lead him to the extremes of diatribe that brought him eventually to disgrace at Pisa and at St. Elizabeths. Pound was a controversialist by temperament, and most of what came to him in his career, both the good and the bad, resulted from his natural contentiousness—combined, of course, with his genius.

His manner most of the time, however, was polite and courtly, and when I finally left him that first afternoon on the grounds of St. Elizabeths, he got up and embraced his wife, kissing her on both cheeks in the European fashion, and saying "Ciao" as they parted.

"You'll come again?" he asked me. "We've got to have some fellows at work, you know: the harvest is plenteous, but the laborers are few. These institutions for the suppression of learning have got it all wrong. They talk about American writers who can't stand comparison with writers of other countries. The literature of this country begins with the Jefferson-Adams correspondence, and goes through Benton, and Del Mar, the greatest American historian, and Agassiz. They produced American literature that meant something, because they were concerned with subject matter, not technique. Get to know David Horton; he's doing something worthwhile. And come back. You can't say everything in one afternoon." He ducked into the door of the building, carrying the lawn chairs and two mesh bags stuffed with books, papers, and food, and waved goodbye.

I drove Dorothy Pound to her cellar apartment near the hospital, and we talked of the possibility that the Eisenhower administration might look favorably on Pound's release, though she was not hopeful, having lived so long with his imprisonment. But she was aware of efforts then being made in Pound's behalf; and during the second term of Eisenhower's presidency, in 1958, the Department of Justice, after much prodding by Archibald MacLeish and Robert Frost, finally agreed to drop the charges against Pound, on the ground that he would never be fit to stand trial. I asked Dorothy Pound how her husband managed to do so much writing in confinement, and she said he was allowed a typewriter and some books, but that Ezra had to give her passages of Chinese to take down to the Library of Congress and look up in the dictionary. She said that Ezra maintained the best way to learn a language was to take certain classic texts and work them over carefully: "You don't have to know everything written in a language, just the best part." I asked her if she had any company when she was not at the hospital, and she said no. "I have a son and Ezra has a daughter, and they keep in touch with us, but we don't see them, because Omar is in England and Mary is in Italy."

I visited Pound a half-dozen times altogether, during May and June of 1955, and I came to feel a real bond of friendship and affection for him, as I think almost everyone who knew him did. The more I talked with him, the saner he appeared to be. He had not lost his sense of humor, and he enjoyed calling himself Grampa and St. Elizabeths the bughouse. One afternoon a member of the circle called his attention to an eccentric-looking woman who was feeding the squirrels, and asked Pound if she were one of the inmates. "No," was the quick retort, "but I think she's responsible for someone's being here." There were some less rational moments, though, when he seemed convinced that he had enemies outside the asylum who were waiting to "get him" if he ever were freed. And though he had frequent Jewish visitors, he sometimes shocked me with an anti-Semitic remark, as when I mentioned the Fugitive poets of Nashville once, and he said, "Oh, yes, they're a talented bunch, but it took a Jew to get them started" (he knew their history well, for a central figure was Sidney Hirsch). He added, as if in defense: "The individual Jew is often a cultural activator, but collectively they have to be watched." Such occasional outbursts reminded me of an observation Hemingway made about Pound during their friendship in Paris in the twenties— that he was either dead right or dead wrong, and it was easy to tell the difference. But they also reminded me that Pound's mind had never been entirely balanced, and his judgment, especially about people, was often untrustworthy—his admiration for Benito Mussolini being the most flagrant example of his misjudgment.

On literary matters Pound was still very much in touch with his age, and his judgment could be astute. He read magazines and books of poems, and sometimes lent me his copy of the *Hudson Review*, or a current book of poems that had been sent to him, following one such gift with a postcard addressed to me which said: "DON't s.v.p. bring any of that stuff BACK. one allus fergits to eggspress some part of one's meaning." He was generally critical of the superficiality of much contemporary poetry, but he mentioned Robert Lowell admiringly, singling out the poem "Ford Madox Ford" (later to appear in *Life Studies*) as a true portrait of a writer he had known well, and who, he thought, was much neglected but due for a revival. He took exception to Possum Eliot's opinion that Milton's poetry, which both Pound and Eliot had deprecated in their early years, might also be due for a revival: "It's still too early to return to Milton," he averred with feeling, as if talking directly to Eliot (and Eliot was among his visitors at St. Elizabeths, I learned from Mrs. Pound). Among recent anthologies he liked Lloyd Frankenberg's *Invitation to Poetry*, which in his opinion contained "more than just yatter." I asked him about Lin Yutang, who was a respected Chinese writer at that time, in the Confucian tradition to which Pound himself belonged, but he was uninterested, saying "he doesn't seem to be a serious character." (After Jim Dickey had been to see him, Pound told me: "We liked your friend Dickey. He looks serious.")

I have learned from the publication of Dickey's and Pound's letters to each other (*Paideuma*, Fall 1982) that their meeting (it was in June—not August—of 1955) led to some spirited exchanges later, and even to a lecture by Dickey on Pound in Pound's native state of Idaho in 1979. My own correspondence with Pound was slighter, though in one of Pound's letters to Dickey he mentioned my "quite bright effusions." I still have his last letter to me, written after I had been discharged from the Navy and had returned with my wife to Nashville to teach and to complete my PhD at Vanderbilt on James, Eliot, and Pound. I had asked him for details of his meetings with Henry James in London, and he replied impatiently:

22 June '57

yu'l have get yr/ memories of H.J. viva voce/
cant stop work to write memoirs.

Cantos 96/105 may shed some light.
in mean time hack away at yr/ iggurunce with
Sq. $ plus Blackstone and the rest of Benton and
Del Mar.

The maximum bestiality is covered by
enc/Int/Txt Bk/ the swinishness of issuing all
new currency as interest-bearing debt. noted by
my grand dad in 1878/ and I think by Mirabeau
and some clean americans from time of Jxn. and
Randolph.

BUT curing one disease is not the COMPLETE
perfection of govt. what have you heard of the
corporate state and vocational representation?

H. J. annoyed me in "youthe"/ and the Turn of
the Screw naturally gets more publicity that [sic]
other books in a polluted age.

The letter was typed, and signed with a flourish EP (the initials
were drawn so as to look like Gaudier-Brzeska's sketch of
Pound's head, often printed on the dust jackets of his New
Directions books). Scrawled below the initials was a further
message: "W. Watt hopes start mag 'Agora' for anagogic archi-
tecture."

Although Pound was ignoring my questions about
writers and responding with pronouncements on his old hobby-
horses of politics and economics, I wrote him again; but he
never replied to my last letter, and I heard only indirectly, from
James Laughlin and Hugh Kenner, that Pound had been pleased
with my anthology *The Imagist Poem*, published in 1963 and
dedicated to Pound. Later I was amazed to discover that in
addition to all the writing and translating he was doing during
the time I visited him, he was writing long letters, almost every
day, to a wide range of correspondents in the United States and
abroad, many of whom were young women who had never met

Pound. Among the unpublished letters at the University of Texas I found some written in May and June of 1955 that mentioned my visits to him at St. Elizabeths. One said cryptically: "Mr. Pratt about to be prof. in Tenn brot Mrs. ditto," and another spoke of "Wm. Pratt doing a thesis and the kulchur hounds faithful with thermos, proper tea but no cups"—references to the social amenities which were observed in the Pound circle. I discovered only one letter with any reference to our conversation: "Mr. Pratt was surprised to hear that Alfafa Bill had heard of Waddell, he (the Pratt) comes from Oklahoma. He had heard of Alfafa but not of Waddell." I had forgotten that Governor William Murray of Oklahoma, nicknamed Alfafa Bill, was one of Pound's interests, and I know only about Waddell what Pound has written about him—my ignorance was constantly exposed in Pound's company: that much I do remember well.

    These letters confirm that I made far less impression on Pound than he made on me, but I learned much from him then, and have gone on learning from him. What strongly remains of those meetings of thirty years ago is the memory of a hearty, unpredictable, stimulating personality, and the imprint of a powerful mind, capable of lucid flashes of insight into literature and history, and of sometimes alarming social and political opinions, who could concentrate his thoughts in conversation and in writing under the most extreme limitations on his personal freedom and his human dignity. What remains in my library, as visible proof of some of the most enlightening and influential encounters in my life, is an inscribed copy of Pound's translation of *The Classic Anthology Defined by Confucius*. On the flyleaf, in his immediately recognizable but barely legible scrawl, are these words:

CERTIFIED TO HV BN IN POSSESSION OF WM PRATT

JUNE 28, 1955

EZRA POUND

(Acknowledgments: Passages from previously unpublished letters by Ezra Pound, copyright © 1985 by the Trustees of the Ezra Pound Literary Property Trust, are used by permission of New Directions Publishing Corp., agents, and by permission of

the Harry Howe Ransom Research Center, the University of
Texas at Austin.)

10

POUND'S HELLS, REAL AND IMAGINARY

When Ezra Pound, as an old man in Rome, was interviewed by Donald Hall for the *Paris Review*, Hall learned that a reporter had once asked where he was living now, and Pound had replied, "In Hell," and when asked "Which Hell?" he put his hand over his heart and answered "Here."[1] Pound, as a major poet who wrote about major themes, and who had the poet's indispensable ear for what he called *melopoeia*, the music of words, included among his major themes the worldly themes he listed in *Canto XI*:

> "*de litteris et de armis, praestantibusque ingeniis*,
> Both of ancient times and our own; books, arms,
> And of men of unusual genius,
> Both of ancient times and our own, in short the usual subjects
> Of conversation between intelligent men,"

But he also included what all major Western poets starting with Homer have included: otherworldly, visionary realms beyond the senses, especially infernal regions, which are found not only in Homer but in Virgil and Ovid, and of course in Dante and Milton. Pound could write of the "Thrones" or heavenly regions as well, but like the greatest poets of every age, he produced more infernal than ethereal images, which only means that evil seemed more real to him than good, or as he might have put it, poets write more often diagnostically, telling us what is wrong with ourselves, than therapeutically, telling us how to make it right. By the end of *The Cantos*, Pound had been forced to recognize that he himself was a "man seeking good / doing evil," and to confess that "my errors and wrecks lie about me," for "I have lost my center / fighting the world." He had, however, in the course of his long career become a major poet because he confronted evil over and over, at his highest moments objectifying it in memorable images of Hell, that incorporate both the real suffering he knew as a man and the imaginary suffering he envisioned as a poet. As Robert Lowell

---

[1] Donald Hall, "Fragments of Ezra Pound," in *Remembering Poets: Reminscences and Opinions* (New York: Harper Colophon Books, 1979) 191.

reported after seeing Pound as an old man in Venice in 1966, "I tried to tell him that he was about the only man alive who had lived through Purgatory, and come through white with a kind of honesty and humility."[2]

Pound admired Dante above all poets, and drew much of his inspiration from Dante's *Inferno*, that Hell of Hells in world poetry, beginning as early as his "Sestina: Altaforte" where, as his epigraph tells us, "Dante Alighieri put this man in hell for that he was a stirrer up of strife. Eccovi! Judge ye! Have I dug him up again?" It is a question most readers would answer in the affirmative, for Pound did achieve his aim of bringing the much-admired Provençal troubadour Bertran de Born to life again out of Dante's Hell. But his imaginary journey to Hell also received early inspiration from the Classical Roman poet Propertius. In two different poems Pound creatively translated Propertius's elegiac Latin into memorable English. The first of these Hell images occurs in Pound's earliest *Personae* volume, dating from 1910:

Prayer for His Lady's Life
From Propertius, *Elegiae*, lib. III, 26

Here let thy clemency, Persephone, hold firm,
Do thou, Pluto, bring here no greater harshness.
So many thousand beauties are gone down to Avernus

Ye might let one remain above with us.
With you is Iope, with you the white-gleaming Tyro,
With you is Europa and the shameless Pasiphae,
And all the fair from Troy and all from Achaia,
From the sundered realms, of Thebes and of aged Priamus;
And all the maidens of Rome, as many as they were,
They died and the greed of your flame consumes them.

> *Here let thy clemency, Persephone, hold firm*
> *Do thou, Pluto, bring here no greater harshness.*
> *So many thousand fair are gone down to Avernus,*
> *Ye might let one remain above with us.*

---

[2] *The Letters of Robert Lowell*, edited by Saskia Hamilton (New York: Farrar, Straus & Giroux, 2005) 470.

This translation is distinguishable from many other Pound translations in his early works in that it takes the subject of Hell seriously and envisions it as a final repository for beautiful women. But when Pound put together a set of translations from the Latin poet in 1917, in a sequence of twelve sections that make up his first long poem, *Homage to Sextus Propertius*, he revised his earlier version considerably and made a better poem of it, fitting it into the longer work as Section IX, Part 2:

> Persephone and Dis, Dis, have mercy upon her,
> There are enough women in hell,
>   quite enough beautiful women,
> Iope, and Tyro, and Pasiphae, and the formal girls of Achaia,
> And out of Troad, and from the Campania,
> Death has his tooth in the lot,
>   Avernus lusts for the lot of them,
> Beauty is not eternal, no man has perennial fortune,
> Slow foot, or swift foot, death delays but for a season.

In this condensed translation of Propertius's Elegy, Hell becomes a more active force of death, a masculine Avernus "lusting" for mortal women whom he carries down to the lower depths, just as Pluto or Dis had carried Persephone to Hell in the Greek myth, and Pound reinforces the theme of mortality by picturing a Hell filled with "quite enough beautiful women," yet still seeking more, seeking even Propertius's mistress Cynthia. So Pound improved upon his earlier translation of Propertius and at the same time increased the potency of his vision of Hell, showing that he had become a more mature poet in the decade between them.

However, the most profound and moving vision of Hell to be found in the *Homage to Sextus Propertius*, and indeed in all of Pound's poetry prior to *The Cantos*, is Section VI, which describes both the dead and the living:

> When, when, and whenever death closes our eyelids,
> Moving naked over Acheron
> Upon the one raft, victor and conquered together,
> Marius and Jugurtha together,
>   one tangle of shadows.
>
> Caesar plots against India,

Tigris and Euphrates shall, from now on, flow at his bidding,
Tibet shall be full of Roman policemen,
The Parthians shall get used to our statuary
                    and acquire a Roman religion;
One raft on the veiled flood of Acheron,
Marius and Jugurtha together.

Nor at my funeral either will there be any long trail,
      bearing ancestral lares and images;
No trumpets filled with my emptiness,
Nor shall it be on an Atalic bed;
The perfumed cloths shall be absent.
A small plebeian procession
Enough, enough and in plenty
There will be three books at my obsequies
Which I take, my not unworthy gift, to Persephone.

You will follow the bare scarified breast
Nor will you be weary of calling my name, nor too weary
      To place the last kiss on my lips
When the Syrian onyx is broken.

      "He who is now vacant dust
      Was once the slave of one passion:"
Give that much inscription
      "Death why tardily come?"

You, sometimes, will lament a lost friend,
      For it is a custom:
This care for past men,

Since Adonis was gored in Idalia, and the Cytharean
Ran crying with out-spread hair,
In vain, you call back the shade,
In vain, Cynthia. Vain call to unanswering shadow,
Small talk comes from small bones.

Pound never worded his description of Hell, or of death, more
vividly anywhere in his poetry than in this section of a poem
which is as much an original as a translation: it is Pound plus
Propertius, the twentieth-century A.D. American poet echoing the
first-century B.C. Roman poet, but adding his own phrases and

twists of irony to the elegant irony of the Latin poet. Rather than picturing the many mythical beauties in Hell, Pound pictures the historical Roman general Marius and his vanquished African opponent Jugurtha, figures out of Roman history in the century before Propertius, but seen as joined in death on the same "raft," that is, on Charon's boat crossing the Acheron to Hell with dead souls aboard it, as it was portrayed by Virgil in Book 6 of his *Aeneid* and again by Dante in the third canto of his *Inferno*, but neither Virgil nor Dante pictured the souls of Marius and Jugurtha on Charon's boat. Pound speaks for Propertius, a dead soul already, who imagines his mistress Cynthia attending his funeral and trying to call him back from the dead, but in vain, since he will be only an "unanswering shadow" then and her plea will be unheard, for—in the moving pathos of the poem—"small talk comes from small bones." Pound has converted Propertius's Classical image of Hell from a place under the earth after death to a state of mind during life, for any who can imagine a Hell before death.

What Pound accomplished in *Homage to Sextus Propertius* brought Hell forward from ancient belief to contemporary relevance, making it personal as well as universal, expressing regret for the mortality of all human beings and at the same time expressing the anticipation of death as a common fate for all who have ever lived, the victorious hero as well as his defeated enemy, the poet as well as his beloved, thus offering some consolation in a death which no one can escape, yet grief nevertheless for the loss of heroes as well as lovers, generals as well as poets. Though Pound subscribed to neither pagan nor Christian religious creed in his depiction of Hell, he was clearly seized with a vision of Hell from his earliest years and it never left him, becoming more and more fully realized in his "forty-year epic" of *The Cantos* which took him from *the Homage to Sextus Propertius* in 1917 to the final *Drafts and Fragments of Cantos CX-CXVII* in 1968.

Pound spoke of having two main themes in his *Cantos:* the descent of a living man into Hell, and the moment of Metamorphosis or vision; in other words, he divided his version of Dante's *Divine Comedy* into two realms, Hell and Heaven, with no Purgatory—unless his Purgatory was a state alternating between Heaven and Hell. Pound had written as early as 1910, in his chapter on Dante in *The Spirit of Romance*, that "Dante conceived the real Hell, Purgatory, and Paradise as states, not places,"[3] and so when he modeled his *Cantos* on Dante's epic poem, he meant his poem to be consistent with Dante as he understood him. Dante, in his view, showed that "Hell is the state of man dominated by his passions, who has lost 'the good of the intelligence.'"[4] In Pound's modern epic, Hell is most often portrayed as a place of darkness governed by men who are driven by "money-lust" or usury, (in 1934, responding to Laurence Binyon's new translation of the *Inferno*, Pound asserted that "the whole hell reeks with money") while Heaven is a place of light governed by a ruler like Confucius or Thomas Jefferson who encourages the arts and philosophy to flourish. To simplify Pound's very complex poem, Hell is damned by money, the material root of evil; Heaven is glorified by art, the spiritual sublimation of good.

   The Cantos begin, not with Dante but with Homer, and specifically, with the journey to Hell of Ulysses in Book 11 of *The Odyssey*. *Canto I* consists mostly of a translation of Homer's Greek, filtered through the medium of an obscure medieval Latin translator named Andreas Divus, and infused with the rhythm of Anglo-Saxon meter, the alliterative four-beat line of *Beowulf* and "The Seafarer" and "The Wanderer":

> And then went down to the ship,
> Set keel to breakers, forth on the godly sea, and
> We set up mast and sail on that swart ship,
> Bore sheep aboard her, and our bodies also
> Heavy with weeping, and winds from sternward
> Bore us out onward with bellying canvas,
> Circe's this craft, the trim-coifed goddess.
>
> *Canto I*

Pound follows Homer's story only so far as Ulysses goes in his journey to receive the prophecy of Tiresias that will guide him in his return to his native island of Ithaca—less than half of Book 11 of *The Odyssey*—but it serves Pound's purpose of descending into Hell with Ulysses so that he, the American poet of the Twentieth Century, can fashion an epic poem that will become his figurative homeland and the fulfillment of his vision. He breaks off the first

---

[3] Pound, *The Spirit of Romance*, 128.

[4] Pound, *The Spirit of Romance*, 129.

Canto by bringing in Aphrodite, the Greek goddess of love, and
the Golden Bough of Argicida, or Hermes, that symbol of
immortality which Aeneas in Book 6 of Virgil's epic, *The Aeneid*,
found with the guidance of the Sibyl of Cumae and the help of his
mother, the goddess Venus, to lead him safely through Hades.
Thus Pound's poem begins with a salute to Homer and an aside to
Virgil, epic poets of Greece and Rome whose heroes Ulysses and
Aeneas had long ago made their mythical journeys to Hell.

Pound was also writing *The Cantos* with Dante in mind,
but he does not bring Dante directly into his poem until *Cantos
XIV* through *XVI*, his Hell Cantos, and *Canto XLV*, his Usury
Canto. He does not stint when he envisions his own imaginary
Inferno, going even further than Dante in portraying the ugliness
of the lower regions: it is thoroughly disgusting, flowing with
excrement and overwhelmed with greed. *Cantos XIV* and *XV*
suffer in comparison with Dante's Hell, because they are
dominated by unrelieved obscenity, "without dignity, without
tragedy," ditches full of besmutted bishops and lady golfers wal-
lowing in slime, but as Eliot observed in *After Strange Gods: A
Primer of Modern Heresy* in 1933: "Mr. Pound's Hell, for all its
horrors, is a perfectly comfortable one for the modern mind to
contemplate, and disturbing to no one's complacency: it is a Hell
for the other people, the people we read about in newspapers, not
for oneself and one's friends."[5] Eliot's remark may have prompted
Pound himself to say in his essay on Cavalcanti shortly afterward
(1934):

> This invention of hells for one's enemies, and
> mess, confusion in sculpture is always
> symptomatic of supineness, bad hygiene, bad
> physique (possibly envy); even the diseases of
> mind, they do not try to cure as such, but devise
> hells to punish, not to heal, the individual
> sufferer.[6]

Apparently Pound realized that he might have gone beyond Dante
in punishing his enemies in *Cantos XIV* and *XV*, moving danger-

---

[5] Eliot, *After Strange Gods: A Primer of Modern Heresy* (New York and

London: Faber, 1934) 43.

[6] Pound, *Literary Essays*, 150.

ously close to the "hell-obsession" he denounced in other poets, but *Canto XVI* is written in another dimension, appearing at first to place him in Purgatory, beyond Hell, but quickly descending again into war as Hell, and specifically, World War I, to which many of Pound's friends went, some of them to be killed. He mentions Richard Aldington, his fellow Imagist poet, and Henri Gaudier-Brzeska, the French sculptor killed in the war, and T. E. Hulme, the founder of the original School of Images, who took library books with him to the trenches—Pound notes in a humorous aside that the library complained—but who also was killed, and then Wyndham Lewis, the editor of the short-lived Vorticist magazine *Blast*. All these fellow-artists were drawn into the folly of war, and Pound's anger is directed at those who led their nations into war and profited from it while many talented men were lost. *Canto XVI* contains deeper human interest than the two preceding Hell Cantos, and is an eloquent protest against war as man's creation of a Hell on earth.

What most creates Hell on earth for Pound is usury, and in *Canto XLV*, he denounces Dante's cursed *Usura*, or excessive profit-making, as materialism or money-worship, and he gives a ringing litany of all the artists whose works were not made for monetary gain but for the love of art and in celebration of the immortal spirit in man. They are almost all Renaissance Italian painters and architects—Pietro Lombardo and Duccio and Piero della Francesca and "Zuan Bellin'" (Giovanni Bellini) and Botticelli and Fra Angelico and Ambrogio Praedis—all, that is, except the anonymous French architects of the Romanesque basilicas of St. Trophime in Arles and St. Hilaire in Poitiers, and the Flemish painter Hans Memling. Pound's poem is a splendid example of the rhetorical technique of *polysyndeton*, or successive and repeated coordination, and it reads like the impassioned denunciation of sin by a Hebrew prophet—he lives up to his name of "Ezra"—but it is largely the exaltation of artists who succeeded despite Usury in creating great works of art—quite different in character from the Usura Canto of Dante, who pictures his sinners suffering punishments in Hell for their unnatural greed, not the blessed who escaped it by their art.

Taking *Cantos I, XIV-XVI*, and *XLV* together to comprise Pound's full image of Hell, we can say that he borrowed from Homer, Virgil, and Dante to portray a composite state of man governed by passion more than reason, mixing mythical as well as historical characters from the past with his own contemporaries in the present, denouncing as sins chiefly the folly and destruction of war and the corruption of greed, but showing the ability of some men to pass through Hell unscathed, like Ulysses and Aeneas in the past and Aldington and Lewis in the present, with Pound himself as artist experiencing but surviving the Hell he creates by his imagination.

Pound added substantially to the earlier Hell Cantos, written mainly in English, with two later Hell Cantos he wrote in Italian during the Second World War. *Cantos LXXII* and *LXXIII* are his nearest equivalents to Dante's *Inferno*, the model for his entire sequence, though Pound's Italian is much more colloquial and much less lyrical than Dante's. The Italian Cantos are most like his own earlier *Canto XVI*, in that war is their major subject, but they are unlike the earlier Hell Cantos in that they focus on particular figures, as Dante did, first Pound's own contemporary and friend, Tomaso Marinetti, the founder of Futurism, in *Canto LXXII*, and then Dante's contemporary and friend, Guido Cavalcanti, in *Canto LXXIII*.

Canto LXXII brings the recently dead Marinetti, who, like Pound, had been a supporter of Mussolini, into ghostly touch with Pound: he audaciously asks for Pound's body to continue his fight. Pound refuses on the reasonable ground that his body is old, and besides he still needs it, but he salutes Marinetti in parting, with the assertion "ch'io faccia il canto della guerra eternal / Fra luce e fango" ("that I have made the song of the eternal war between light and mud") and wishes him a hearty farewell, "Addio, Marinetti!" The remaining lines bring in other figures, but not so vividly: Sigismondo da Malatesta and Galla Placidia from earlier cantos, and Ezzelina da Romano from Dante's *Inferno*, all of whom confirm that the war is still going on and that he must continue to sing about it.

Canto LXXIII allows Pound to bring back to life Guido Calvacanti, much admired and translated by Pound early in his career. Cavalcanti appears as a ghost on horseback ("Cavalcanti" means "horseman" in Italian) and tells Pound that he has ridden past Rimini, where Sigismondo's Tempio is threatened by the advancing Allied armies, and has seen a young Italian woman heroically avenge her rape by a troop of Canadian soldiers, dying with them in a minefield explosion into which she leads them: "All'inferno 'l nemico, / furon venti morti, / Morta la ragazza" ("twenty dead enemy soldiers sent to Hell, and the girl dead, too"), "ma che ragazza!"—"but what a girl!" he exclaims admiringly—and then Cavalcanti recalls where he has come from, "Io tornato son' / dal terzo cielo" ("I have returned from the Third Heaven") of Venus, still marveling at the bravery of the Italian girl he has seen on the battlefield of the Second World War.

The Italian Cantos carry forward Pound's imagery of Hell into the later Cantos, but the culmination of it is to be found in the *Pisan Cantos*, where the imprisonment of Pound himself in the army detention camp at Pisa, "a lone ant from a broken anthill," gives the most compelling sense of the state of man "dominated by his passions, who has lost 'the good of the intelligence" as was true of the lost souls in Dante's *Inferno*.

Pound's moving account of his humiliation and physical suffering as a traitor places him by inference in the Ninth Circle of Dante's *Inferno*, where traitors like Count Ugolino (who betrayed Pisa) become cannibals, through forced starvation in the tower where they are kept, and Judas and Brutus and Cassius writhe in the mouth of Satan. Pound does not literally compare himself, as a traitor to his country, to these arch-traitors in Dante's poem, but the analogy cannot escape those who read Pound with Dante in mind. Finally, however, Pound is able by the power of his imagination to transcend his real, earthly Hell, and rise to the moving affirmation in *Canto LXXXI*:

> First came the seen, then thus the palpable
> Elysium, though it were in the halls of hell,
> What thou lovest well is thy true heritage.

Pound, in other words, was able through his imagination to find a place of blessedness in a place of torment, just as Aeneas in Virgil's epic found Elysium in Hades, a Heaven in the midst of Hell. Furthermore, Pound can attest in lines of exquisite lyricism that poetry, "what thou lovest well," is possible even in the worst conditions imaginable, as he proved by the superb poetry he wrote at Pisa and later in the asylum of St. Elizabeths in Washington, among them the lines of *Canto XC* of "Section: Rock-Drill," where "out of Erebus, [another name for Hell] the deep-lying / from the wind under the earth, *m'elevasti*," that is, "I lift myself up"—further proof of Pound's astonishing ability to transcend his personal and real Hell. As quoted earlier, H. D. would later attest in her tribute, *End to Torment: A Memoir of Ezra Pound*, "There is a reserve of dynamic or daemonic power from which we may all draw. He lay on the floor of the iron cage and wrote the *Pisan*

Cantos."[7] Pound's triumph over adversity comes through his poetic gift, in spite of his shame and his madness:

> To have gathered from the air a live tradition,
> Or from a fine old eye the unconquered flame,
> This is not vanity.
>
> *Canto LXXXI*

Like earlier epic poets who wrote of Hell, like Homer and Virgil and Dante, Pound made poetry out of his own physical and mental torment, and he presents an original and forceful modern image of Hell, above all in the *Pisan Cantos*, where the power of his imagination enables him to envision "Elysium, though it were in the halls of hell."

Of course, it can be said that Pound never really transcended Hell, that is, Evil and Death and Madness. To those who visited him during his long stay at St. Elizabeths, he liked to refer to himself as "Grampa in the bughouse," and he admitted in the last *Drafts and Fragments of Cantos CX-CXVII* that he became in his old age a "blown husk that is finished," who like Ulysses has "lost all companions," just as Tiresias in Hades had predicted for him in *Canto I*. In fact Pound in the end was less like Homer's Ulysses, who emerged alive from Hell and returned alone to his home in Ithaca, than like Dante's Ulysses, who in *Canto XXVI* of the *Inferno* sails from Ithaca into unknown seas, beyond the Gates of Hercules, and is shipwrecked and drowned at the foot of Mt. Purgatory, having exceeded the limitations set for mortals, and instead of being rewarded for his daring is placed in one of the lowest regions of Hell, not among the fallen heroes in Purgatory or the saints in Paradise. As Pound told Donald Hall in his *Paris Review* interview in 1960, "It is difficult to write a paradiso when all the superficial indications are that you ought to write an apocalypse. It is obviously much easier to find inhabitants for an inferno or even a purgatorio."[8]

Pound never finished his poem, and so he never achieved Dante's redeeming vision of Heaven as the Heart of Light. He seems to have left himself in the Heart of Darkness, consigned

---

[7] H. D., *End to Torment*, 44.

[8] *Writers at Work: The Paris Review Interviews, Second Series* (New York: Viking Press, 1965) 56.

without redemption to the lowest region of Hell, where he placed himself by inference in the *Pisan Cantos*. But no reader can forget that Pound had the power to imagine Heaven even in Hell, and so, if he admitted "Many errors,/ a little rightness, / to excuse his [Dante's] hell / and my [Pound's] paradiso," he ended his epic with a touching prayer of penitence:

> Let the Gods forgive what I
>
> > > have made
> > > *Notes for CXVII et seq.*

Pound's Hell was both real and imaginary, and it lasted all the way through *The Cantos*, but he could still speak wistfully at the end:

> about that terzo
> > > third heaven,
> > > > that Venere
> again is all "paradiso"
> > > > a nice quiet paradise
> > > > > over the shambles
> > > > > *Canto CXVI*

And he could plead, as if preparing to face the Last Judgment:

> that I tried to make a paradiso
> terrestre
> > > *Notes for Canto CXVI et seq.*

So perhaps in death, if not in life, he could say as he has the ghost of Guido Cavalcanti say in *Canto LXXIII*: "Io tornato son' / dal terzo cielo"—"I have returned from the Third Heaven."

CONCLUSION

BEYOND MODERNISM: EZRA POUND AS VATIC POET

"Vates cum fistula" or "Prophet with a Boil," Pound called himself in 1922, when he returned the manuscript of *The Waste Land* to T. S. Eliot, edited down to about half its length, "in the form in which it now appears in print" according to Eliot. Pound took no credit for the poem, saying he had simply performed a "Caesarean Operation" on it, that he was just the "Sage Homme" or "Male Midwife," his title for the satirical poem he sent to Eliot with the edited manuscript. It was an inside joke, but there was meaning as well as humor in it, since Pound was indeed an irritable prophet. Plato had said in *The Republic* that poets were not to be trusted as rulers of the state, because their utterances were oracular rather than rational. Plato wanted his ideal republic to be ruled by philosopher-kings; therefore poets were to be outlawed, though he often quoted Homer in his dialogues as a mark of respect for the sort of wisdom that he knew poets were capable of uttering. It was Plato's teacher, Socrates, who compared teachers to midwives, revealing to others what he said they already knew, helping them recover the wisdom which the soul possessed from a previous existence. This doctrine of "recollection," or reincarnation, was not foreign to Pound, who, as we have seen, had, in one of his earliest and most revealing poems, "Histrion," declared that living poets may reincarnate dead poets, citing Dante and Villon as poets whose souls sometimes possessed him:

> No man hath dared to write this thing as yet,
> And yet I know, how that the souls of all men great
> At times pass through us,
> And we are melted into them, and are not
> Save as reflections of their souls.
> Thus am I Dante for a space and am
> One Francois Villon, ballad-lord and thief ...

What the Greek philosophers had propounded, Pound brought to life. He became both a great poet and a great teacher of poets. He wrote major poems himself, and he served as midwife to other great poets like Eliot. As both poet and teacher, Pound has few rivals among world poets. But it must be admitted that he did not always live up to his potential: he was at times a bad poet and a poor teacher. Brilliantly successful in teaching other writers how to Make it New, how to be Modern, he was a failure at teaching anyone about economics and politics. Randall Jarrell gave him credit for being "the education of poets," the mastermind who led a revolution in literary style early in his career, inventing new ways of using words that influenced more than one generation of writers. He was so successful, W. H. Auden once said, that no one writing English in the twentieth century could be sure that he hadn't been influenced by Ezra Pound. But he was far from effective as a teacher later in his career, when he tried to extend his influence beyond the literary sphere, with his embarrassing and ill-tempered ravings over Rome Radio during the Second World War. His claim that he was only practicing free speech, as guaranteed by the American Bill of Rights, was not valid in Fascist Italy, a wartime enemy of the United States, and it is no wonder that he was arrested, imprisoned, and indicted for treason by his own countrymen, having proved himself an untrustworthy citizen of the state he constantly professed to love but never ceased criticizing.

It could be said that for all his wisdom, Pound justified Plato's exclusion of poets from his Republic, since he confirmed the opinion that poets are irrational, not philosophers but oracles, who speak with a divinely (or in some cases demonically) inspired voice. Pound did not shrink from casting himself in such a prophetic role, as we know from another early poem, "Scriptor Ignotus" ("Unknown Writer"):

> From out the heights I dwell in, when
> That great sense of power is upon me
> And I see my greater soul-self bending
> Sibylwise with that great forty-year epic
> That you know of, yet unwrit …

The "forty-year epic" was of course *The Cantos*, his longest and most ambitious work, and in it, as in much of his writing, early and late, Pound clearly spoke as a prophet as well as a poet. He was at his best a true prophet, but a false prophet at his worst. He left to his readers the task of distinguishing the true from the false prophet, as they have been trying to do ever since. It isn't easy, because the work of Ezra Pound, more than that of any major poet, forces the reader to reject the worst he wrote in order to concentrate on the best. He could make that distinction admirably for other writers like Eliot, but he seemed unable or unwilling to do so for himself. He was massively, aggressively human, as much the victim of his own excesses as the acknowledged master of many languages and a verbal magician. Verbal magician he was, sometimes uncontrollably, throughout his long life. He poured out more words in public and in private than any major writer. Besides the sheer bulk of his poetry and prose, his enormous correspondence already runs to many volumes, and there are many more unpublished letters still to be edited. He was like an unstoppable verbal fountain, spewing out a stream of words that might range from the depths of vulgarity to the heights of eloquence. To say he was both prophet and poet is to agree with Plato that the poet is not fully in control of the wisdom (or vituperation) he articulates; he is a Sibyl who waits for a god or a goddess (or a demon) to speak through him. "I believe in the gods," Pound said when pressed by Eliot to say what he really believed in. His gods might be named Christ or Dionysus and his goddesses might be named Aphrodite or Mary, but they were real to him, whatever their names, and he sometimes fused them, envisioning Christ and Dionysus as one sacrificial god and Aphrodite and Mary as a single love goddess, whose song, "La donna è mobile," Pound delighted to hear, as he often did, played by the sexton on the bells of San Pantaleo, the little church above Rapallo where Pound lived for many years with his mistress, Olga Rudge, the mother of his child, whose name happened to be Mary. Pound's vision at its best incorporated heaven and earth, as in *Canto LXXXI* of *The Pisan Cantos*, written in the Hell of the Pisan prison camp, which opens with the marriage of Heaven and Earth: "Zeus lies in Ceres' bosom." But though Pound was not Homer—nor Dante, nor Villon, his other favorite poets—he at times could match the expressive power of their words with his own eloquence. It was his pioneering work, and the encouragement he gave to other writers of genius, that largely created Modernism as a movement. More than any other writer, he led the effort to "resuscitate the dead art / Of poetry," and became indisputably one of the great poets in world literature, whatever else he might have been in his turbulent, controversial lifetime.

Pound could not have achieved as much if he had not taken on the role of prophet as well as poet. He had deliberately set out to know world poetry better than anyone, and his success was confirmed by many other poets, notably by Yeats, who was older, and Eliot, who was younger. If his knowledge of poetry often seemed miraculous and unaccountable, it enabled him not only to write great poetry himself but to help others write it, too. "It is tremendously important that great poetry be written," as he said in "A Retrospect" in 1918, summing up what the revolutionary movement he called Imagism had accomplished in a decade, but "it makes no jot of difference who writes it." His theory of poetry was consciously impersonal; his practice of it was inevitably personal. He had the gift of discerning which writers of the present and of the past really mattered, whether they wrote English or another major language, and he knew other languages well enough to translate some of their best poetry into comparable English poetry. As early as 1910, in *The Spirit of Romance*, he held that where poetry was concerned, "all ages are contemporaneous," and that an intelligent reader should be able "to weigh Theocritus and Yeats in the same balance."

To read Pound is inevitably to weigh *him* against other great poets, a critical act in itself, because one must adopt his practice as a reader, being ready to recognize true poetry wherever it appears, often in the midst of unworthy verses that surround it. Like all great poets, Pound demanded intelligent readers, but more than other great poets, he demanded that his readers not only try to understand him but distinguish his best work from his worst. Of his voluminous output, much is highly poetic, but much, alas, is unpoetic; it is up to each reader to sift the wheat from the chaff. It is a constant challenge to read Pound, for every reader is obliged to deal with Pound's work as he dealt with Eliot's, separating the lines of genuinely inspired poetry from what is often a welter of artificial or uninspired verses. An alert reader can see that Pound often missed the mark, but that when he hit it, he hit it with resounding force. What Hemingway said about him was true, that Pound was dead right half the time and dead wrong half the time. Pound wrote poetry by intuition, not reason, and sometimes he himself was not sure of its worth. At his best, he had the eyes of a seer and the voice of a prophet, and could

produce lines of such commanding authority that it is impossible
to deny their rightness, so that the reader feels compelled to join
him in asking, "What whiteness will you add to that whiteness,
what candor?" Yet his words are full of ambiguity; they resonate
in the mind; their meaning is always elusive, defying complete
explication. His poetry at its best issues forth Sibyl-like, with the
power of revelation, and it is not too much to say that Pound saw
the world apocalyptically, envisioning both the beginning and the
end of time.

Pound was a tragic poet, finally, and he wore the tragic
mask most often in the *Pisan Cantos*. But his apocalyptic vision is
to be found in the early poetry as it is in the late. One of his
Imagist touchstones, "The Return," dramatically changes its
French source, from an image of nameless gods alive and active
in the natural world into the Greek gods returning like weary
hunters from the chase. They seem hesitant, lacking the will to
persevere, but Pound leaves no doubt that they are vividly present
to his eyes: "See they return," he says, and he bears witness that
"These were the "Wing'd with Awe," "Gods of the winged shoe!"
even if their hounds have become "slow on the leash" and they
themselves faint—"Pallid the leash-men." Yeats used this poem to
preface the revised version of *A Vision*, his most prophetic book,
because he said it expressed better than any of his own poems the
view that the cycles or gyres of history repeat themselves in new
forms, and that what seemed an end might also be a beginning.
Pound first saw the gods returning in a single short poem, but he
came back to it in a poem of greater length, near the end of his
career, when in *Canto CXIII*, the most memorable of his final
Drafts and Fragments, he declared, consciously echoing his
earlier poem:

> The Gods have not returned. "They have never left us."
> They have not returned.

These very early and very late poems span his career, and the
prophetic vision is Pound's own. He *sees* the gods, visible as well
as invisible, and he witnesses their return at first hand, even if
other men miss seeing them, or doubt whether they ever existed.
Together, the poems show that Pound had the capacity for
reverence, even awe, and that, sophisticated though he was, he
was sometimes smitten by the undeniable power of the miraculous, essential to the prophetic voice at any time or place, which

he felt modern civilization was losing. "People who have lost reverence have lost a great deal," he lamented late in his life.[1] The prophetic voice in his poems could be his own, though more often, it was the voices of gods or of men long dead, and their invisible presence was with him from the very outset of his career, when he testified in *The Spirit of Romance*:

> For our basis in nature we rest on the indisputable and very scientific fact that there are in the "normal course of things" certain times, a certain sort of moment more than another, when a man feels his immortality upon him.[2]

He went on to say that "the forms of ecstatic religion," which included Christianity, had ritualized this feeling of immortality, of timeless existence, so that it could be expressed in religious worship as well as in poetry. But for Pound, the moment of immortality was clearly the moment of poetic inspiration.

To be a prophet in the popular sense is to "predict the future," but in the literal sense, derived from the Greek προφήτης, it is to "speak for" someone else, especially to take the role of human interpreter of the divine will, to be oracular, and Pound in that sense was often prophetic, often speaking for someone other than himself. That someone else might be a divine or a human agent. Pound's theory of the *persona* or mask allowed him to speak for a variety of beings, real or imagined, different from himself and different from each other. At times he could declaim like a Hebrew prophet, as in *Canto XLV*, denouncing what he called usury or money-madness vehemently in verse after verse, while at other times he could speak with courtly politeness, as in *Canto XXXVI*, in the soft tones of an earlier poet, Cavalcanti, about the refinements of love. To call Pound a vatic poet is to place him outside the traditional role of the prophet, the voice of God speaking to men, for his voices might be those of dead heroes like Confucius or Jefferson, or dead poets like Homer or Dante, embodying their spirits as he employed their words, which he quoted or translated or imitated in his work. Whatever mask he

---

[1] Pound, *Paris Review* Interview, 52.
[2] Pound, *The Spirit of Romance*, 94.

wore, Pound himself was always there behind it, incorporating the spirits of the dead in the language of the living, whether speaking through a comic or a tragic mask.

Pound took on the role of the vatic poet most often in *The Cantos*, for there, in contrast to his earlier finished poems, he wrote as if in a continuous sequence or flow of poetic utterance, that started with *Canto I* and never stopped, only pausing between the numbered Cantos for breath, letting them trail out with ellipsis marks rather than ending them with a definite period. His chief model was Dante's *Divine Comedy*, with its hundred cantos, but they were a unified whole, visionary and prophetic and carefully composed, shaped in a symmetry of hendecasyllabic verses from canto to canto, and guided from beginning to end by devout Christian belief. The 117 cantos of Pound's long poem, in contrast, appear to have a beginning but no middle or end, no common measure of length, no consistent poetic form, no over-arching theme, and many different gods and goddesses. Pound was polylingual and polytheistic, and he deliberately created the effect of a continuous utterance spoken by many different voices, sometimes his own but sometimes identifiably different. His own voice asserts itself especially in the climactic sequence of the *Pisan Cantos*, from *Canto LXXIV* to *LXXXIV*, where it is most often a tragic voice behind a tragic mask. Any reader familiar with the poem as a whole is bound to be aware, not only of Pound's different voices, but of differences in the quality of individual Cantos, and in the best of them what he hears most often is the voice of the vatic poet.

The best of *The Cantos*—what are they? It is not easy to say. Each reader must make his own choice, since Pound left no clues as to which he preferred. Though some cantos have been quoted more often than others, there is as yet no definite consensus about which are best. It is true that in the broken continuity of more than 800 pages of poetry, certain cantos are more unified and more expressive than others, but we know that Pound himself had trouble deciding which were best. He made a false start with the first three cantos he published in 1917, wisely deciding to revise and reorder them when he published a longer sequence, which he called *A Draft of XVI Cantos*, in 1925. Here was the real beginning of what his subtitle called *A Poem of Some Length*. It was a "Draft," rather than a set of finished poems. It remained a draft to the very end, more than forty years later, because he never really completed it. Pound had long projected

"that great forty-year epic," but he wrote it piecemeal, a few
Cantos at a time, and treated it as a work continually in progress.
All he managed to give it was a definite beginning, with the
newly fashioned first Canto taking precedence over all the others.
There, at the beginning, Pound spoke with the voice of Homer, by
a masterful translation (with the help of a Latin crib) of the
opening passage of Book 11 of *The Odyssey*. Thus, from the
beginning of his major lifework, Pound chose to speak for
someone other than himself, and what he chose was the mask and
voice of Homer's hero, Ulysses. He had used Ulysses as an alter
ego earlier when he wrote his ironic self-portrait, *Hugh Selwyn
Mauberley*, where it was a metaphor for the poet in quest of a
reputation, but in *Canto I* it is Homer's Ulysses, describing in his
own words his sea voyage to Hades, the World of the Dead,
where he has been sent by the sorceress Circe, who had
imprisoned him and his men for a year on her island, in order to
hear the prophecy of Tiresias, the mythical Greek seer, who alone
can tell him how to sail homeward to Ithaca, avoiding many perils
on his journey and eventually reaching home ten years after the
Greek victory in the Trojan War. This Homeric passage has long
been called the *Nekuia*, or Book of the Dead, because it describes
the elaborate steps Ulysses must take to summon dead spirits,
according to Greek religious rites, and it is traditionally thought to
be the oldest poem in any Western language, and so the very
beginning of Western literature. Pound clearly meant his first
Canto to start where the Western literary tradition started, with a
prophetic as well as a poetic vision. As Pound later told his father,
his opening theme was a "Live man goes down into world of
Dead,"[3] in order to learn how to complete the journey of his life.
The speaker is Ulysses, but Pound is behind the mask, figuratively
taking up Ulysses' journey to follow his own career as a poet. We
know that Pound is there, listening, when Tiresias asks Ulysses
why he has come to the World of the Dead:

> "A second time? why? Man of ill star,
> Facing the sunless dead and this joyless region?"

Since Ulysses traveled to Hades only once, Pound is conscious of
repeating the feat poetically. He was well aware that the
metaphysical descent into Hades, or Hell, or the Underworld, was

---

[3] Pound, *Letters*, 210.

central to epic poetry, not only as it began with Book 11 of Homer's *Odyssey*, but later with Book Six of Virgil's *Aeneid* and the entire Inferno of Dante's *Divine Comedy*. So when Ulysses has performed the rites, and Tiresias delivers his prophecy, he is speaking to Pound as well as to Ulysses.

> "Odysseus
> "Shalt return through spiteful Neptune, over dark seas,
> "Lose all companions."

Pound would quote some of these words much later, in the midst of a Hell he could not have foreseen, the American prison camp at Pisa. He could hardly have anticipated the tragic events of his own life, but in *Canto LXXIV*, the first of *The Pisan Cantos*, he saw that he had, fortuitously, fulfilled the prophecy of Tiresias, because by then he had outlived all his old friends, the great writers he knew in London in the second decade of the twentieth century, who with him had made Modernism into a major literary movement:

> Lorldly men are to earth o'ergiven
>   these the companions:
> Fordie that wrote of giants
> and William who dreamed of nobility
>   and Jim the comedian singing:
> "Blarrney castle me darlin'
> you're nothing now but a StOWne"

Ford Madox Ford, William Butler Yeats, James Joyce—these were the writers Pound remembered in the depth of his humiliation at Pisa, just as Ulysses remembered his shipmates when he returned without them to Ithaca. In *Canto I*, Pound was consciously continuing the tradition of the poet as prophet for a new age.

That *The Cantos* have a beginning is the most definite thing about the whole poem. They have no real middle or end; instead, they have scores of brilliant lines, flashes of genius which illuminate the mind of the reader and remain with him as only great poetry can. Some individual cantos have a semblance of unity, but for the most part the 117 cantos are unequal and arbitrary; what arrests the reader's attention and lingers in his memory are many striking individual lines and passages, often less integral to the canto in which they appear than to the continuity of the poem as a whole. These lines may and often do emanate from a godly or ghostly presence, the persona Pound chooses to invoke in any given canto. He invoked many personae, donned or doffed a succession of masks, in no logical association or chronological sequence, but at will, as it pleased him to imagine himself speaking for them. This vatic role was so natural to him that some of the voices become personalities inside the poem, independent of their sources in history or literature. Listed in order of their appearance, they would make up a sort of Pantheon of Gods and Heroes in *The Cantos*, Pound himself among them (just as Dante is one of the heroes of *The Divine Comedy*):

> Ulysses (*Canto I*)
> Dionysus (*Canto II, Canto XVII, Canto LXXIX*)
> Eleanor of Acquitaine (*Canto VI*)
> Henry James (*Canto VII*)
> Sigismundo Malatesta (*Cantos VIII-XI*)
> Confucius (*Canto XIII*)
> Thomas Jefferson (*Canto XXI*)
> John Adams (*Canto XXXI*)
> Guido Cavalcanti (*Canto XXXVI*)
> Pound at Pisa (*Cantos LXXIV-LXXXIV*)
> Osiris and Adonis (*Cantos XCI-XCIII*)
> Apollo and Artemis (*Canto CIII*)
> Pound's Farewell (*Fragments of Cantos XV-XVI*)

The list is not complete, nor does it include all of the best Cantos, but it does suggest that Pound, in his role as vatic poet, dramatized a strange assortment of divine and human figures, bringing them to life briefly and memorably, often in their own words. His own prophetic voice is dominant in the climactic sequence of *The Pisan Cantos*, where, by common consent of readers and critics, the poet reaches the summit of his powers, creating poetic lines that reverberate in the mind of the reader long afterward. These are the most quotable cantos, and by that measure the best, and the voice that speaks them is mostly Pound's own voice. This voice, issuing out of the worst possible physical circumstances, where the poet has been condemned to suffer as a prisoner in an open cage, surrounded by guards and other prisoners, is often poignant with regret, yet is nevertheless capable as Pound was of creating magnificent imagery and of speaking with exalted eloquence.

The *Pisan Cantos* open tragically, for the first words are about "The enormous tragedy of the dream in the peasant's bent shoulders," (*Canto LXXIV*) expressing regret for the unfortunate people of Italy, who lived and died under Fascism without seeing its humanitarian goals achieved, and they go on to describe what Pound personally lived through, arrested by his own people and subjected to the punishment reserved for the most hardened and dangerous criminals:

> they digged a ditch round about me
> lest the damp gnaw through my bones
> > > *Canto LXXIV*

He sees himself as condemned, "a man on whom the sun has gone down," (*Canto LXXIV*) a casualty of the collapse of Western civilization,

> As a lone ant from a broken ant-hill
> From the wreckage of Europe, ego scriptor.
> > > *Canto LXXVI*

He speaks of himself in the third person, in *Canto LXXIX*, as he seeks a night's rest on the floor of his prison cage, invoking the gods of the Dawn and the Dusk:

> > Old Ez folded his blankets
> Neither Eos nor Hesperus has suffered wrong at my hands

He willingly admits his arrogance, "I have been hard as youth sixty years," (*Canto LXXX*), and knows he is the cause of his present disgrace, condemning himself in the voice of the Biblical prophet Ecclesiastes:

> > Pull down thy vanity
> Thou art a beaten dog beneath the hail,
> A swollen magpie in a fitful sun,
> Half black half white
> No knowst'ou wing from tail
> > > *Canto LXXXI*

In *Canto LXXXII*, he has a brief premonition of the end of his life:

> the loneliness of death came upon me
> (at 3 P.M., for an instant)

and he pleads wearily at the end of *Canto LXXXIII*, "Oh let an old man rest." But Pound concludes the entire set of the *Pisan Cantos* with an image of himself as a stubborn survivor, who will not give up the struggle to go on living despite all the adversity he has suffered, most of it brought on by his own intemperance, who is now grateful simply to be alive:

> If the hoar frost grip thy tent
> Thou wilt give thanks when night is spent.
> *Canto LXXXIV*

These confessional lines are moving in their self-torment, but they were not his only voice at Pisa. There were other times in the prison camp when Pound proved that he still had the keen perception and gift for verbal imagery that characterized his best poetry, that he was resilient enough to rebound from the most degrading circumstances and envision "Elysium, though it were in the halls of hell." As a prisoner kept outside, exposed to the elements, he had learned to appreciate the simplest pleasures of life:

> there was a smell of mint under the tent flaps
> especially after the rain
> and a white ox on the road toward Pisa
> as if facing the tower
> *Canto LXXIV*

And at times, in a tone of wonder, he observes the small miracles of nature:

> Hast 'ou seen the rose in the steel dust
> (or swansdown ever?)
> *Canto LXXIV*

(Here Pound was borrowing a line from Ben Jonson's poem, "Her Triumph":

> Ha' you felt the wool of beaver,
> Or swan's down ever?

altering the context without naming his source.)

He could admire unashamedly the daily panorama of natural beauty—"sunset grand couturier" (*Canto LXXX*)—or patiently observe the motions of the tiniest fellow creatures:

> Brother Wasp is building a very neat house
> of four rooms, one shaped like a squat Indian bottle
> > *Canto LXXXIII*

and above all, he could feel the restorative power of the natural world:

> When the mind swings by a grass-blade
> an ant's forefoot shall save you
> the clover leaf smells and tastes as its flower
> > *Canto LXXXIII*

And notably, despite his confinement and humiliation at the age of 60, Pound never lost his sense of humor. He believed that "the virtue *hilaritas*" had helped him survive the worst life could offer, and that the ability to laugh, whether at himself or at others, enabled him to avoid sinking into the depression and despair that would have been normal to most human beings. He listened to the banter of his fellow Americans, guards as well as prisoners, and, as a man of many words himself, noted that their language was limited to a mouthful of profanities and obscenities:

> The army vocabulary contains almost 48 words
> One verb and participle one substantive
> One adjective and one phrase sexless
> That is used as a sort of pronoun
> From a watchman's club to a vamp or fair lady
> > *Canto LXXVII*

He sometimes reported verbatim and without comment the insults they hurled at each other:

> "Hey, Snag, what's in the bibl'?
> What are the books of the bibl'?

> Name 'em! Don't bullshit me!"
> *Canto LXXVII*

And he listened indulgently to one prisoner's halting attempt to make music:

> Mr. G. Scott whistling Lili Marlene
> with positively less musical talent
> than that of any other men of colour
> whom I have ever encountered
> *Canto LXXIX*

The "men of colour" were American blacks, and since all the prisoners at Pisa were black except himself, he enjoyed imitating the American Negro dialect for comic effect, just as Mark Twain might have done:

> "ah certainly dew lak dawgs,
> ah goin' tuh wash you"
> (no, not to the author, to the canine unwilling in question)
> *Canto LXXIX*

But he was equally capable in other moods of mocking the pretensions of his venerable friend, the distinguished Irish poet and senator, William Butler Yeats:

> And Uncle William dawdling around Notre Dame
> In search of whatever
> Paused to admire the symbol
> With Notre Dame standing inside it
> *Canto LXXXIII*

For all his moments of brooding introspection and acute observation, interspersed with sudden bursts of humor, in the somber setting of the Pisan prison camp, there were moments of sudden visionary experience which are among his most memorable passages. He was definitely the vatic poet when he imagined the cliff overlooking the sea at Terracina, south of Rapallo, with its ruined temple dedicated to Aphrodite, the Goddess of Love, a vanished shrine which he hoped to see restored some day:

till the shrine be again white with marble
till the stone eyes look again seaward
                        The wind is part of the process
                        The rain is part of the process
                                Canto LXXIV

He recalled Cavalcanti's ballad of love, which he had translated
long before in *Canto XXXVI*, with its reminder that

                Nothing matters but the quality
        of the affection—
        in the end—that has carved the trace in the mind
        dove sta memoria
                                Canto LXXVI

He remembered, too, this time not mockingly but convivially,
how Yeats had looked out over the rooftops of Rapallo with him,
more than a decade earlier,

        "Sligo in heaven" murmured Uncle William
                when the mist finally settled down on Tigullio
                                Canto LXXVII

The whole of *Canto LXXIX* is a poetic apostrophe addressed to
the lynx, the sacred beast of Dionysus, with a rhythm beating time
to the ritual dances performed in worship of the Greek gods, both
Zagreus (Dionysus), the god of ecstasy, and Aphrodite, the
goddess of love:

                O lynx, keep the edge on my cider
                Keep it clear without cloud...
        ....
        Therein is the dance of the bassarids
                Therein are centaurs
        And now Priapus with Faunus
                The Graces have brought Αφροδιτην
        Her cell is drawn by ten leopards

                O lynx, guard my vineyard
                As the grape swells under vine leaf
                                Canto LXXIX

So Pound's vatic voice in the *Pisan Cantos* varies from visionary poetry about gods and goddesses, to realistic natural imagery, to satire, and even to farce. The dominant setting is the American prison camp at Pisa, though he remembers nostalgically other times and places, especially London early in the century, when he presided over the birth of Modernism with Yeats and Eliot and Joyce. The Army DTC around him may have been unrelievedly grim; his immediate environment in the open cage or the medical tent may have been ugly, and his treatment may have been harsh; nevertheless, in the worst circumstances of his life, Pound wrote some of his finest poetry. He had the power to speak through the tragic mask in the midst of his darkest hours.

When he reached the summit of his eloquence in *Canto LXXXI*, the most often quoted and praised of all *The Cantos*, the role of the vatic poet is most evident. It is a relatively short canto, but it is clearly oracular and impossible to paraphrase. It is full of quotable lines that are not logically consecutive; in fact, they have almost nothing in common except that they all issue from the same mind. He starts with a commanding image of the marriage of Heaven and Earth, "Zeus lies in Ceres' bosom," which is purely visionary, but he quickly descends to the mundane with youthful memories of Spain on a 1906 visit, remembers the paintings of Velazquez he marveled at in the Prado, makes a passing reference to Franco, the Fascist dictator of Spain following the Spanish Civil War in the 1930s, and then brings up a bewildering assortment of names of those he knew at different periods, English, French, and American (among them "Possum," the nickname T. S. Eliot liked so well he adopted it for his lighter poems about cats). Quite suddenly, in the midst of these random recollections, he sums up in a single line the achievement of Modernism: "To break the pentameter, that was the first heave." He then remarks, without transition, what is happening around him in the prison camp: "thank Benin for this table ex packing box," made for him by a friendly black prisoner, who warns Pound "doan yu tell no one I made it," implying that it was a forbidden gift. He follows with a mental image of "George Santayana arriving in the port of Boston," the Spanish philosopher speaking with a Castilian lisp, which Pound arbitrarily associates with Mussolini's use of the Roman "u" for "v"—"a grace quasi imperceptible." None of these associations are logical; they are Pound's mind subjectively at work on his experience, mixing the past and the present freely, alternating formal English with colloquial English, bracketing the trivial with the significant. But Pound was moving in his whimsical way toward two of his finest lyric passages, the chief reasons why *Canto LXXXI* has drawn high praise from every reader. The first lyric begins "Yet ere the season died a-cold" and is a tribute to what might be called the genius of English poetry and music, again loosely paraphrasing Ben Jonson in the line, "Hast 'ou fashioned so airy a mood," and honoring in its refrain two Elizabethan composers, Henry Lawes (who set Waller's "Go, Lovely Rose" to music) and John Jenkins, coupling them arbitrarily with Arnold Dolmetsch, whom Pound knew in London, a maker of ancient instruments on which these songs might be played:

> *Lawes and Jenkyns guard thy rest*
> *Dolmetsch ever be thy guest*

This inspired lyric passage shows Pound in full poetic power, generating verbal music in stanzas that almost sing themselves, exemplifying and at the same time paying tribute to the greatness of the English musical and poetic tradition, past and present.

But the final lyric is even better. Since it was first published in 1948, it has been so often quoted as to have entered into the English language permanently, along with Chaucer, whom it paraphrases, and the Book of Ecclesiastes in the King James Translation, which supplied the refrain, "Pull down thy vanity." It begins with "What thou lovest well remains," and it exquisitely characterizes what Pound loves, the long, rich heritage of beauty and poetry, while it castigates his faults—all the vanity, hatred, and falsehood. It ends memorably with what he insists were positive achievements in spite of his faults, which brought about the revolution in literary style we call Modernism:

> To have gathered from the air a live tradition
> Or from a fine old eye the unconquered flame

Pound had not brought Modernism into being singlehandedly, of course, but he had led the way, and his closing lyric in *Canto LXXXI* is fine enough to redeem all 117 cantos—all the wrongheadedness, the wordiness, the incoherence. It is the best proof of his poetic wisdom, and it is uttered prophetically. Reading this climactic canto confirms the fact that Pound knew how to write great poetry but was not always in control of his gift.

He proved that Plato was right in believing poets to be oracles more often than philosophers. When Pound wrote lines of surpassing eloquence, as he often did, the gods or dead heroes and poets spoke through him. When he faltered, as he often did, his vanity misled him. At his worst he was mistaken; at his best he was inspired. If he had been able to condense *The Cantos* into their best lines, as he once did for Eliot when he edited *The Waste Land*, they would be universally recognized as his masterpiece—fragmentary, yet powerfully expressive. They are his masterpiece anyway, because they are nobly tragic in their best utterance, filled with the knowledge of personal suffering and cultural loss caused mainly by war. Pound's most memorable lines are clearly vatic; they speak in words about a reality beyond words, adopting both godly and human voices, with his own inimitable voice distinct among them.

If Pound can be called a vatic poet at his best, so can Yeats, so can Eliot, so can Joyce, so can Faulkner. These five masters of Modernism all wrote intuitively and prophetically about the age they lived in and the world they inhabited. Modernism in literature favored both the prophetic voice and the apocalyptic vision, and its greatest writers spoke with a wisdom that transcends the age. Faulkner once said that one should read Joyce's *Ulysses* as a backwoods Baptist preacher reads the Bible: with faith. He could have said the same of his own work, especially novels like *The Sound and the Fury*, *As I Lay Dying*, *Absalom, Absalom!*, *The Bear*. Pound did not write the sort of stream-of-consciousness fiction Joyce and Faulkner invented, but he wrote what could be called stream-of-consciousness poetry, and he launched a Modern movement that included both fiction and poetry. His Imagist movement led the way to a new literary style, and its poetic theory was more oracular than philosophical. It insisted that reality was subjective, discrete, and disjunctive, rather than logical or chronological. Its principle was that "the image is the speech." What Pound promoted from the beginning was poetry that came from a momentary revelation, a sudden flash of insight, not from a narrative sequence. It was the representation in words of a reality beyond words, filled with the apocalyptic vision of the poet. Pound understood that "to maintain 'the sublime' / in the old sense" meant to find new forms of expression for what were permanent truths of human experience, to concentrate meaning into language so that it would penetrate into both the subconscious and superconscious regions of the mind. There the poet might speak with a wisdom beyond understanding, and Modernism might go beyond what the age demanded, generating great literature out of a violent and chaotic period of history.

LIBRARY, UNIVERSITY OF CHESTER

BIBLIOGRAPHY

Berryman, John. *The Freedom of the Poet.* New York: Farrar, Straus & Giroux, 1976.

Blackmur, R. P. *Form and Value in Modern Poetry.* New York: Doubleday Anchor Books, 1957.

Carpenter, Humphrey. *A Serious Character: The Life of Ezra Pound.* Boston: Houghton Mifflin, 1988.

cummings, e. e. *The Selected Letters of e. e. cummings.* Edited by F. W. Dupee and George Stade. New York: Harcourt, Brace & World, 1969.

Davie, Donald. *Two Ways out of Whitman.* Edited by Doreen Davie. Manchester: Carcanet, 2000.

Doolittle, Hilda (H. D.). *End to Torment: A Memoir of Ezra Pound.* New York: New Directions, 1979.

Eliot, T. S. *After Strange Gods: A Primer of Modern Heresy.* New York and London: 1934.

———. "American Literature and the American Language," first published in St. Louis in 1953, reprinted in *To Criticize the Critic.* New York: Farrar, Straus & Giroux, 1965.

———. *Collected Poems, 1909-1962.* New York: Harcourt Brace Jovanovich, 1969.

———. "Ezra Pound (1946)" in *A Collection of Essays to be Presented to Ezra Pound on his 65th Birthday.* Edited by Peter Russell. London: Peter Nevill, 1950.

———. Review of *Baudelaire and the Symbolists* by Peter Quennell, in *Criterion* IX (Jan. 1930): 359.

———. *The Selected Letters of T. S. Eliot.* Vol. I, 1898-1922. Edited by Valerie Eliot. New York: Harcourt, Brace, Jovanovich, 1988.

————. *The Waste Land, A Facsimile and Transcript of the Original Drafts, including the Annotations of Ezra Pound.* Edited by Valerie Eliot. New York: Harcourt, Brace, Jovanovich, 1971.

Ellmann, Richard. "Ez and Old Billyum" in *Eminent Domain: Yeats Among Wilde, Joyce, Pound, Eliot and Auden.* New York: 1967.

Fenollosa, Ernest. "The Chinese Written Character as a Medium for Poetry." Edited by Ezra Pound. First published in 1920. Reprinted San Francisco: City Lights Books, 1936.

Flint, F. S. Unpublished draft of an article on Imagism written about 1918, on file in the Humanities Research Center at the University of Texas, Austin, Texas.

Hall, Donald. "Fragments of Ezra Pound," in *Remembering Poets: Reminiscences and Opinions.* New York: Harper Colophon Books, 1979.

Hulme, T. E. "Notes on Language and Style," in *Further Speculations.* Edited by Sam Hynes. Minneapolis: U. of Minnesota, 1955.

Jarrell, Randall. "Fifty Years of American Poetry," in *The Third Book of Criticism.* New York: Farrar, Straus & Giroux, 1965.

Kenner, Hugh. *The Pound Era.* Berkeley: U. of California, 1971.

————. "What Prison Taught the Poet," review of *Ezra and Dorothy Pound: Letters in Captivity, 1945-46*, in *The Wall Street Journal* (Feb. 5, 1999): W 10.

Lattimore, Richmond. *Greek Lyrics.* Chicago: U. of Chicago, 1960.

Lowell, Robert. *The Letters of Robert Lowell.* Edited by Saskia Hamilton. New York: Farrar, Straus & Giroux, 2005.

Middleton, Christopher. "Documents on Imagism from the Papers of F. S. Flint," in *The Review*, No. 15 (Apr. 1965): 35-51.

Nicholls, Peter. *Modernisms: A Literary Guide.* Berkeley: University of California Press, 1995.

Obata, Shigeyoshi. *The Works of Li Po, The Chinese Poet.* New York: Paragon, 1965.

Pound, Ezra. *The Cantos of Ezra Pound.* New York: New Directions, 1995.

————. *The Collected Early Poems of Ezra Pound.* Edited by Michael John King. New York: New Directions, 1976.

————. Coltrane, Robert. "The Imagist Relationship between Pound's 'Les Millwins' and Eliot's "Morning at the Window" in *Paideuma*, 18, 3 (Winter 1989): 123-28.

————. *Ezra Pound Perspectives: Essays in Honor of his Eightieth Birthday.* Edited by Noel Stock. Chicago: Henry Regnery, 1965. Reprinted Westport, CT: Greenwood Press, 1977.

————. *Gaudier-Brzeska.* New York: New Directions, 1960.

————. *Guide to Kulchur.* New York: New Directions, n.d. First published in London in 1938.

————. *The Letters of Ezra Pound, 1907-1941.* Edited by D. D. Paige. New York: Harcourt Brace, 1950.

————. *The Letters of Ezra Pound to Alice Corbin Henderson.* Edited by Ira Nadel. Austin: U. of Texas, 1993.

————. *Literary Essays of Ezra Pound.* Edited by T. S. Eliot. New York: New Directions. 1954.

————. *Paris Review Interview* in *Writers at Work, Second Series.* New York: Viking, 1965.

————. *Personae: The Collected Poems of Ezra Pound.* New York: Boni & Liveright, 1926.

————. *Personae: The Shorter Poems.* A Revised Edition by Lea Baechler and A. Walton Litz. New York: New Directions, 1990.

————. "Vorticism" in *Fortnightly Review* XCVI, 1 (Sept. 1, 1914): 461-71.

Pratt, William. *The Imagist Poem: Modern Poetry in Miniature* New York: Dutton Paperback Originals, 1963. Revised and expanded edition, Ashland, Oregon: Storyline, 2002.

Ransom, John Crowe. "New Poets and Old Muses" in *Selected Essays of John Crowe Ransom.* Edited by Thomas D. Young and John Hindle. Baton Rouge: Louisiana State, 1984.

Riding, Laura and Graves, Robert. *A Survey of Modernist Poetry.* First published 1928, reprinted New York: Haskell House, 1969.

Spender, Stephen. *The Struggle of the Modern.* Berkeley: University of California Press, 1963.

Taupin, René. *The Influence of French Symbolism on Modern American Poetry.* Translated by William Pratt and Anne Rich Pratt. New York: AMS Press, 1985.

Warren, Robert Penn. "Tribute to Ezra Pound." Radio broadcast for his seventieth birthday, Dec. 1955. A transcript of this broadcast from Yale University is on file in the Humanities Research Center at the University of Texas, Austin.

Woolf, Virginia. "Mr. Bennett and Mrs. Brown," in *The Captain's Death Bed and Other Essays.* New York: Harcourt Brace, 1950.

Yeats, William Butler. *A Vision.* Reissued with the author's final revisions. New York: Macmillan, 1966.

————. *The Autobiography of William Butler Yeats*. New York: Doubleday Anchor Books, 1958.

————. *Essays and Introductions*. New York: Macmillan, 1961.

————. Excerpts from a speech by Yeats published in *The Egoist* (Feb. 2, 1914): 57.

————. *The Letters of William Butler Yeats*. Edited by Allen Wade. New York: Macmillan, 1955.

————. *The Uncollected Prose of W. B. Yeats*. Edited by John P. Frayne and Colton Johnson. New York: Macmillan, 1975.

————. Variorum Edition of *The Plays of W. B. Yeats*. Edited by Russell Alspach. New York: Macmillan, 1969.

————. Variorum Edition of *The Poems of W. B. Yeats*. Edited by Peter Allt and Russell K. Alspach. New York: Macmillan, 1965.

INDEX